EMBRACING SUSTAINABILITY

A Warning and a Guide
For the Future of Humanity

Marc C. Seamon, Ph.D.

Copyright © 2015 Marc C. Seamon
All Rights Reserved. No part of this book may be reproduced in any form or by any electronic or mechanical means, including information storage and retrieval systems, without permission in writing from the publisher.

Visit Embracing Sustainability on Facebook for more information.

ISBN 978-0-9968940-0-5

For Brighton and Christopher

CONTENTS

Preface	7
Why Sustainability?	8
Recipe for Disaster	10
How Long?	13
Resource Friction	15
Top Obstacles to Sustainability	18
Landfills and Human Shame	35
Pride in Our Species	37
Dual Perspectives—Evolution and Conservation	42
Wisdom versus Waste	45
The Peace of Loneliness	49
Steady State Economics	52
A True SFI	54
Have You Ever Wondered?	57
Evenflow or Evanesce	58
A Bug's Life	60
Sustainability and the Passenger Pigeon	62
Time to be Smart	69
Coal is Murder	70
Ground to Dust	72
Earth and Space	74
Falling Apart at the Seams	77
Sustainability and Medicine	79
A Model Life	81
None Quicker Than Ours	95
Unnatural	96
Ungrateful	97
Unqualified	99
Why Not Always?	100
Better Days	101
Rare Earth, Precious Earth	102
Recycled Mistakes	104
Better by design	106
Why Now, Why Us?	107
What Remains	111
Toilet Paper	113
A Sense of Entitlement	114
Fading to Gray	115
Not Our Good Side	118

Campsite Blues	120
What Are You Going to Do With It?	122
On Our Best Behavior	124
The Importance, Complexity and Fragility of Soil	126
All That's Lost	129
Too Big to Handle, But Not Too Big to Fail	144
For Better or Worse—Determinism, Free Will and Social Change	145
Saving What?	147
Flour Power	148
A Long Journey	150
The Hard Way, the Easy Way, or the Right Way	152
Strange Loyalties	153
A Chance	156
Something to Fear	158
Parallel Comprehension	160
The Illusion of Abundance	163
Prisoners unto Ourselves	164
Awareness and Action: Still Disconnected	166
Where the Wild Things Are	167
Sustainability Is Morality	168
Kindness Is Sustainable	169
The Media and Sustainability	170
Sustainability and Education	172
There Is No Sustainable Development	177
The Right Side of the Road	178
Individualism Is Not Sustainability	179
Beyond Sustainability—Striving to Contribute as Planetary Citizens	181
Copyright Permission Acknowledgements	183

Preface

Sustainability

"I can explain it to you, but I cannot comprehend it for you."

Definition of Sustainability:

Sustainable (adj.) or *sustainability* (noun) denotes a lifestyle that could be maintained permanently without becoming untenable because of attributes that are only feasible temporarily. A sustainable existence is one in which no aspect of our individual lives or societal operations would accrue any long-term detriment to life on Earth if exercised indefinitely. More specifically, sustainability implies that humanity should exist in a way that does not depend on finite resources, does not use renewable resources faster than they can be naturally replenished, does not produce waste of a kind or quantity that the Earth cannot absorb without harm, does not adversely impact the right of other living things to flourish on this planet, and ensures that all future life will inherit a planet that is no less rich and functional than nature will allow. A sustainable society is one that meets these standards not grudgingly, but willingly, out of gratitude and reverence for the Earth and its resources. Sustainability must come from the heart if it is to last and must be motivated more by a desire to achieve something good than to avoid something bad.

Understanding the above definition is easy. Recognizing all the ways in which our actions violate its doctrines will take a bit more work for most people. The goal of this book is to help people think in terms of sustainability—to help them recognize the unsustainable practices that are all around them and embrace sustainability as the only feasible model on which to build an existence that will last.

Why Sustainability?

Sustainability is the perfect metric against which to evaluate our activities and lifestyles. Because the word sustainable, by definition, cannot be applied to anything that cannot be maintained indefinitely, it serves as a perfect model and the perfect reminder of what must be achieved, on both an individual and a societal level, if our species is to survive.

The word sustainability is terribly misused. People employ it all the time to refer to things that are absolutely unsustainable in every way. The other day I saw a plastic bottle with a label that indicated it contained 25 percent less plastic than previous bottles of the same size. This reduction in plastic content was touted as being part of a sustainability initiative of some kind. No company that sells its products in plastic bottles can rightfully claim to be doing business sustainably, but many such claims are made all the time.

Corporations and universities love to tout their sustainability plans. Many have them, but I've never seen one that comes close to achieving true sustainability. In fairness, it is probably impossible for any school or business to be truly sustainable today because as a society, we have not developed sustainable pathways. Instead, we have created ways of meeting our needs that are not sustainable. Doing so has resulted in a perplexing conundrum and put us in the frustrating position of finding that the very things we must do to survive (eat, drink, have shelter, create and possess various goods and services to support our lives, work together in an organized society) are themselves the biggest threat to our survival. Talk about a catch 22, the things we do to live are threatening our ability to live. That unpleasant reality exists because modern society was developed through choices made based on convenience and profitability. The people directing the development of society (usually powerful elites in business and government) as well as the rank and file citizens who followed their lead were very shortsighted. Innovations were everywhere, but none of them seemed to have been conceived with sustainability in mind. The first ground rule of developing a complex society should have been to make sure that it was sustainable. But our society was created with no real thought to the future. Instead, instant gratification was the primary motivation, and new developments in technology and lifestyle were embraced as quickly as they could be achieved, regardless of long-term feasibility.

Just as an inexperienced and imprudent tinkerer might race forward in assembling a device without regard for the directions, our forbearers leaped into an industrial revolution and threw together an ill-conceived and dysfunctional society that was (and is) like a machine working against itself. Such a flawed design will not last long before self-destructing. But intelligent engineering could design a machine to serve the same purpose but in a way that will not destroy itself. We needed intelligent engineering at the helm when the complex societies of the world were being developed. Instead, the only theorizing and planning went into developing political systems such as socialism, communism and democracy and the economic system of capitalism, all of which fail to give rise to sustainable societies because they were not designed with that function as a goal. Perhaps the word sustainability could be the name for a new political/economic system that would actually work as a means of plotting a successful path for society.

Recipe for Disaster

The common life of the average American is an absurdly unsustainable folly that no clearly thinking person could view as "normal." We wake up to an electronic alarm clock and rise from a mattress and box spring assembly made of synthetic fibers. Before we've even moved an inch, our lives have required the existence of that clock and bed, which together contain (or required during production) enough toxic material to kill us if taken into our bodies. But it's not in our bodies. It's just absorbed by the planet, so we think it's OK.

We get up and move about a 2,600 square-foot home constructed of unsustainable materials manufactured in an unsustainable way and powered by the extraction and burning of fossil fuels. We begin our daily use of 90 gallons of potable water, much of it we heat with fossil fuels and contaminate with unnatural chemicals before we send it out of our homes to again become part of the natural world, taking our toxic, over-consumptive legacy with it.

We dress in plastic clothes and sit down to eat food (breakfast) grown, packaged, transported and sold in unsustainable ways. When it's time to leave, we put our 200-pound bodies into vehicles weighing 2,000 to 6,000 pounds and then use fossil fuel to generate enough energy to move the entire load (of which our body weight is only 2.5 to 10 percent) to wherever we work. There we do jobs that for the most part involve or promote the overconsumption of natural resources. Then we do the whole thing in reverse, driving back home, eating, watching TV or using other electronic appliances. Oh and don't forget to take out the garbage (30 pounds per person a week of completely avoidable waste destined for the landfill) before going to bed. At almost no time during this day do we stop using energy and/or requiring the overconsumption of natural resources to support our existence. Even while we sleep, we use (and waste) energy.

If the average American life described above sounds utterly normal, conventional and familiar, then you are deluded and blind to the absurdity of our present situation. We are living in a way that cannot possibly be maintained more than perhaps a few hundred more years before it collapses under its own enormous weight. And despite being intelligent enough to perfect the technological marvels of our age, we seem unable to comprehend the absurdity of our own condition. Consider the extravagance of the average American home. No other animal on Earth builds such an elaborate home. Compared with other animals, we require the greatest input of natural resources to support. We are the neediest in terms of what it takes to subsidize our existence. And yet the shamefully extravagant dwellings we build and fill with material items are not permanent. Few houses, nor the stuff we put in them, remain after 100 years. Those making it to 200 years end up on a register of historic places. That the kind of human housing we currently use is renewed in less than 100 years for every person living in developed "first world" nations is completely unsustainable. How can such a practice be maintained for very long?

We have only been building houses similar to the kind we know today for a few hundred years, and only on the scale we see in urban/suburban areas for about 150 years. If population growth continues at its current rate (or even if population levels off), how many humans will have lived in developed parts of the world over the next 100,000 years? Let's say an average of five billion people are alive and living developed lifestyles at any given time during the next 100,000 years, and that the average human lifespan ends up being 100 years. That's housing for five trillion people over that time. Putting it another way, if the average home lasts 100 years before being torn down (most won't last even that long), and an average of five people live in that house during its service life, one trillion homes will be demolished and rebuilt over the next 100,000 years. That's 1,000,000,000,000 homes or 3,333 houses for every person living in America right now. Change the numbers to reflect the current lifespan of around 75 years and a human population level of 8 billion, and 10.6 trillion homes will be needed over the next 100,000 years. That's more than 35,000 homes—a city—for each person alive in America today. Considering how little residential demolition debris is recycled, where will the raw materials for this come from, and what landfill space could possible hold it all after the fact?

It is unimaginable to suppose that humans in the future will be able to continue living as we do today. It is an impossible proposition, requiring too great an input of natural resources, yet most people, if they think about it at all, seem to believe life will go on as it has, with continued increases in technology and invention, indefinitely. If forced to confront these facts, many will say, "Yes, but we'll figure out a way to solve those problems when we get to them." Well, the problems are here now, facing us today. So why wait to being solving them? I am not proposing that we go back to pre-industrial lifestyles. That, too, is impossible. The answer is intelligent and careful social planning. Sustainability will involve increasing efficiency, curtailing extravagance and reducing human population, through attrition, as soon as possible. Such a proposition would be rejected by many as repressive, but there are already plenty of ways in which being part of an organized society can feel restrictive. We must pay taxes and obey laws, go to school, have a driver's license (try doing much without one) and a social security number. Even when we die, the law requires that a licensed mortician examine our body and issue a death certificate before we can be interred. We cooperate with lots of requirements to be part of an organized society, even if it wasn't

Embracing Sustainability

our choice to be born into it. Why, then, is it sinister or unreasonable to suggest that to ensure the survival of our species, we adopt policies regulating sustainable practices and population levels? Is the collapse of our entire civilization a better alternative? To willfully make the latter choice is suicidal, but plenty of people (addicts of all kinds) can't help themselves from throwing away their futures for what they perceive as satisfaction now. Is that to be our collective fate as a species? Such would be a sad and ironic end for the most intelligent species to ever live on Earth.

How Long?

The content of this book suggests that to be truly sustainable, a policy or practice would need to be able to be applied "forever." If it would fail at any point before "forever," then by definition it is an unsustainable action. Forever, by definition, is infinite, which is a quantity that cannot be measured. The Earth will only exist for perhaps another four billion years. It will be a place that can support life for even less time than that. So clearly, "forever" is a needlessly long metric by which to measure sustainability, at least if it is taken literally. A more accurate timeframe would be to say that an action is sustainable if it can be maintained for a duration equal to our natural lifespan as a species.

The average species of mammal on Earth exists for 10 million years before going extinct or becoming a new species through evolution. Some last much longer than 10 million years. Crocodiles and cockroaches have been around for hundreds of millions of years. Whether we want to be around as long as the average species or whether we want to go down in evolutionary history as one of the longest lived ones, we had better plan on our lifestyles being doable for many millions of years. Given that we've been around as a species for 200,000 years now, and living an industrialized lifestyle for about 250, we have a long way to go. If we end up lasting as long as the average species of life on Earth, then we are only .02 percent into our "life," and our industrial lifestyle, which is the cause of so much detriment to ourselves and other life on Earth, accounts for only .000025 percent of the lifespan we might hope for.

To put those numbers into perspective, if the "lifespan" of the human race were reduced to the lifespan of an individual human, say 90 years, then we, as a species, are only 20 months old right now. We've been living an industrialized lifestyle for only about 19 hours. Basically, we've just begun our lives. But already, there are serious signs that we won't be around much longer. It's the equivalent of an infant being born with such massive birth defects that the doctors say there is no chance he will see his first birthday. Likely, he only has days to live. Ninety years is unthinkable. So how long for us? It depends on how seriously we take the notion of sustainability and on the timeframe we envision when we invoke the word. How long, indeed.

We aren't used to thinking about our actions or policies in timeframes lasting hundreds of thousands or millions of years, but there is no good reason not to, unless we fully expect to check out as a species before then. Much of what we do as a society is driven by industry and government. Industry will look into the future only far enough to discern the profitable from the unprofitable. If industry is currently immersed in a profitable situation, it will not look to the future at all.

Our government is simply an aggregation of politicians and bureaucrats. They tend not to think beyond the next election cycle and are definitely not fond of thinking about the future in ways that might make their constituents uncomfortable. So with the major drivers of our society hopelessly mired in the present, there is little chance of us considering the long-term feasibility of anything we do as a species.

Although we humans are self-aware and intelligent, we don't think about the future much better than any other animal on Earth. Like a deer or a rabbit or a turkey, we merely live in the moment and do what satisfies us now. We worry about tomorrow only when it gets here, and we leave the future to take care of itself. This naïve, even fatalistic outlook might be all simple beings need, but we humans are at the helm of a complex and powerful civilization that is capable of doing serious harm to this planet if mismanaged. Our complicated society contains too many variables to leave the future to chance. The only sane approach is one of careful, prudent planning. We need to be thoughtful about the future and always err on the side of caution when uncertain of how some action or policy might play out over time. How long do we have before it's too late to embrace sustainability? How long, indeed.

Resource Friction

Unmitigated friction will eventually destroy anything it acts upon. Given millions of years, even something as gentle as rain can wear down a mountain. Erosion is the work of friction compounded over time.

Physicists tell us there is no such thing as a machine that is 100 percent efficient at transducing energy into power. There is always energy lost, in part to friction. Engineers know this unavoidable friction can destroy the machines they build, so they design them to minimize and manage friction to allow the machine to survive for what is seen as an adequate service life. The pistons and cylinders of an engine that receives regular oil changes will outlast the rest of the car they are in, but if run without oil, they won't last a minute. Friction will destroy them.

Door hinges may creak without oil, but given the small degree of movement they must endure, they don't really wear out and fail from friction during their normal lifetime. The threshold separating an acceptable amount of friction from an unacceptable, destructive amount depends on the application in question and the length of time said application must be supported.

All living things need natural resources in order to survive. Like a machine, living things create some degree of what could be called "resource friction" through the process of taking and using natural resources. This resource friction wears down the systems that produce natural resources. Renewable resource systems can regenerate themselves and repair damage caused by resource friction. As long as the damage occurs more slowly than the healing, the whole process of utilization and replacement is sustainable. If not, it is destined to collapse.

All of our problems with sustainability stem from resource friction. Not only are we using renewable resources faster than they can regenerate, we have also created a lifestyle that depends on the consumption of finite resources that cannot regenerate themselves at all. We also produce waste that cannot be re-assimilated into the natural cycle of use and renewal. To continue with the analogy of engine cylinders, not only are ours running without lubrication, we have thrown in a handful of sand to expedite the wear and tear. The terribly dysfunctional system we have built is facing imminent doom. It is a bad machine that is destroying itself at a frightening rate. It is loud and dangerous, and we should be afraid of it. Just as someone would run away from a steam engine that was about to blow up, we should have a mortal fear of the monster we have created.

But most people seem to have little or no sense of this resource friction. Even as they live unsustainable lives, they are numb to the sensation of resource friction that is grinding and grating relentlessly all around them.

But to those who are attuned to it, the warning sounds and smells are as unmistakable as those of a badly tuned engine to an ace mechanic. Gaining an awareness of the resource friction associated with living goes hand in hand with fine-tuning our society and our individual lives to embrace sustainability. The closer we come to achieving a sustainable existence, the more resource friction will abate. As we solve our biggest problems, resource friction will drop dramatically. As we whittle away at the many smaller obstacles standing between us and sustainability, the resource friction associated with our existence will fade to a tolerable hum, benign background noise that is no more dangerous or threatening than that of any other living thing on Earth. Like the "friction" that emanates from a well-tuned musical instrument, the "sounds" generated by our existence will blend with those of the rest of Earth's inhabitants to finally become a pleasant and positive part of the chorus of life, the voice of a planet.

If it sounds as if resource friction is an indicator of how well we are doing at living in harmony with the planet, you are right. Right now, we are very much out of harmony. As a result, just living our day-to-day lives creates terrible friction and turmoil within the systems that enable life (our own and that of other species) on Earth. It's not just our reliance on finite resources or our overharvesting of renewable ones that creates all this resource friction. Our lifestyles are so extravagant as to seem absurd in comparison with those of other living things on this planet. How can our lives possibly justify the shameless largess most people in "developed" nations flaunt as they barrel onward in our throwaway culture? Each of us, in just the few short years of our lives, extracts so much of value from the planet and expels back into it so much that is harmful as to make it hard to fathom that it is basically unintentional, the side-effect of pursuing comfort, convenience and profit.

The incredible resource friction that accompanies our lifestyle does not need to be multiplied by large magnitudes of time to become unsustainable. The devastation it wreaks on natural systems whose clockwork is calibrated by evolutionary, even geologic time scales is breathtaking. In 200 to 300 years or less, we have corrupted the air, water, soil and biosphere over large tracts of the planet. Our actions have been the equivalent of a bomb blast, ripping apart their surroundings so fast there hasn't been time to notice what is happening. In a microsecond of the Earth's life, we have unleashed intolerable changes within its systems. Why can so few of us perceive the effects of our actions? Why can't we see, hear and feel the resource friction our lifestyles generate as we rip through the bounty of the Earth?

Much of what we know, we know because of signals we receive through our senses (touch, sight, hearing, smell). Gaining a sense of awareness for the resource friction our existence creates would be a tremendously beneficial aid in our quest for sustainability. It's hard to fix a problem you cannot see or hear or feel. Without those senses, it's hard to know the problem is there at all. Resource friction is all around us. Our own lifestyle generates enough of it to rock our planet to its core. It's time we noticed the very real signals of the unsustainable lives we lead.

Top Obstacles to Sustainability

There are dozens of topics or issues that people say need to be addressed in the pursuit of sustainability. Climate change and recycling seem to be the ones that get the most attention, but that doesn't make them the most important. Of the numerous issues we recognize as obstacles to sustainability, which are the most critical? Which ones would we benefit the most from solving? I believe there are three top obstacles facing us. Admittedly, two of my picks are compilations of several issues usually addressed separately, but I believe it makes more sense to see them as related parts of a whole.

1) Overpopulation

Overpopulation is the single biggest problem we face. Unfortunately, it may also be the most difficult to solve, not because the solution is difficult, but because persuading people to enact that solution might prove impossible.

As I write this, world population stands at seven billion. When that figure was reached several months ago, the mainstream media were nearly unanimous in framing it as a positive development. Some places celebrated the seven-billion mark as a great achievement or a victory of some kind for the human race. An unwitting newborn was randomly selected from somewhere and symbolically given the dubious honor of being the world's seven billionth human. It, of course, was not. The seven billionth human would have been born and died long ago. This was merely the first time seven billion of us were all alive at the same time. But I shouldn't say "merely," because that—hitting the seven-billion mark—is a huge problem for us. Our society and our lifestyle make it very easy to ignore the overpopulation problem, but I cannot overemphasize how truly urgent it is. We are facing an extreme emergency, and none of several likely outcomes are pretty. While it might not be obvious to the average person going about his or her life, our population growth over the last 300 years has accelerated so rapidly as to literally defy description. Words cannot do justice to the terrifying reality of what is happening to us. Our population growth is so out of control as to be beyond dangerous. It is a population emergency, and we must react now. We have to begin allowing the human population to decrease immediately. It cannot wait another generation or two.

To those who don't believe there is a problem with overpopulation, I offer the following mathematically derived truths: If the human population would continue to grow as it currently is, by the year 3237 (1,225 years from now), there would be 1.6 quadrillion people on Earth. There are also 1.6 quadrillion square feet of dry land on Earth, so that would mean each person would have to exist within a 12-inch square of real estate. People literally would have to sleep standing up because there would not be enough room to lie down! Try crowding people into those dimensions the next time you are with a group of folks willing to partake in such an experiment. The most common size of floor tile is 1 square foot, so try configuring 25 people into a section of floor measuring five tiles by five tiles. You will find that while your feet can fit into the square, your upper body will be in contact with those of the people on all four sides of you, and it can be difficult or impossible for the people on the outside to even keep their balance and remain upright in their squares. Hopefully, anyone (even overpopulation doubters) considering the scenario of 1.6 quadrillion people would instantly discount it as ludicrous. There would be no way to even approach such a number, as the Earth simply could not provide the resources necessary to support that many people, even if they could all theoretically fit on its surface. With nothing but wall-to-wall humans, there could be no plant or animal life of any kind, and thus no food. Obviously, our population will never grow to 1.6 quadrillion. The question then becomes, "What will stop our numbers and when?"

Those who applaud population growth and say it isn't a problem don't want to hear the answers to the "what" and "when" questions posed in the previous sentence. Their ignorance cannot be allowed to block the way to progress on the most critical problem facing humanity today. The truth they don't want to hear is that our current population of seven billion is already way over the limit of what the Earth can support. Our planet cannot feed, water, power, outfit, equip or absorb the waste of seven billion people permanently. To do so temporarily is requiring us to consume not just the interest but the principal of the Earth's resources. The party can't last, and anyone who says it can is dangerously wrong.

Another misconception doubters of overpopulation in the United States often offer up is the notion that while world population might still be growing, America's is not. That is simply wrong (and even if true, would be irrelevant because it's world population that counts, not just that of a single country). According to the Statistical Abstract of the United States, which is a project of the US Census Bureau, there is one birth in America every eight seconds, one death every 13 seconds, and one net international migrant every 44 seconds. That means that when deaths and emigration are accounted for, the US population is still growing by one person every 15 seconds. That means that the current US population of about 318 million will grow to over 400 million before 2040 and break 500 million by 2055. America is still very much a part of the world's population crisis.

A considerable amount has been written, both in print and on the web, claiming the overpopulation crisis is a myth perpetuated by ill-informed alarmists or fear mongers. These myth theories suggest that 1) human population is already on its way down and will settle at an appropriate level with no help or worry needed from us and 2) overconsumption, not overpopulation, is the problem, and that if we would dispense with our extravagant and wasteful lifestyles, all would be well. Believing in either of these myth theories is dangerous. Our numbers are not on the way down. As evidenced elsewhere in this chapter, human population is growing almost everywhere, and at a rate that is beyond alarming. In mid-2015, the United Nations released population projections for each decade from now until 2100. The numbers, which were revisions of estimates released in 2013, showed that population growth will likely be even greater than anticipated just a few years ago. According to the UN, world population will hit 11.2 billion by the year 2100. Human population and the overall rate at which it is growing just keep going up every year. But even if they weren't, seven billion is not sustainable, regardless of lifestyle. Even if the developed world would rid itself of fossil fuels and plastic and every other extravagant trapping of modern life, there simply is no way the Earth can produce enough food for that many humans indefinitely. Just doing so for a few decades has resulted in deep cuts into biodiversity, water shortages and serious depletion of the topsoil in our best farming areas. How could anyone think we could live this way forever? Such a false hope is completely out of touch with reality.

Another less common but related claim is that the Earth has plenty of good farmland that isn't even being used. A lot of the Eastern United States, these claims assert, was farmed during America's early years but was retired from agricultural use as the frontier moved west and big farming took root on the Great Plains. All of the small, Eastern farms that used to feed families and small communities could easily be put back into production. This, the argument goes, would somehow result in sustainability, but such a position is seriously shortsighted. First, the Great Plains have that name for a reason. They are unparalleled as farmland. The small farms of the East cannot begin to compare to the productivity of the American and Canadian prairie. That's why farming has gravitated to that region. Putting Eastern farms back into production would make only a fractional increase in food production, and without institutional reform, would be no more sustainable than the status quo. Second, needing to put every square inch of farmable land into production is a move of desperation, not sustainability. To live right, we need to be able to do so comfortably off just part, not all, of our potential resource base. Third, a lot of the Eastern farmland that was pastoral and productive 100 years ago is now buried under subdivisions and strip malls, lost as a natural resource that could feed humans or any other life.

When world population exceeded seven billion, I didn't hear a single mainstream media outlet treat the issue as the catastrophe it is. Because the media set the agenda for public discourse, I doubt too many water-cooler conversations lamented the sad harbinger seven billion represented for humanity either. In fact, I doubt there were too many water cooler conversations about the issue at all. In addition to celebratory coverage, I noticed a sizeable portion of media coverage framing the issue in a dry, uneventful sort of way, sending the message that the information was neither that interesting nor that important. Nowhere was it covered as the bad news that it was. It seems as if overpopulation is the last conservation issue most people want to hear about. Any reporter, from local all the way up to major market national correspondents, could have easily found a scientist to interview about the dangers seven billion poses for us. Maybe one did somewhere, but I saw no such report. I hope this will change when the consequences of overpopulation begin to hurt badly enough that no one can ignore the problem. Perhaps there will be more soul-searching and less celebrating when the eight-billion mark is reached. Perhaps we will rue the day nine billion is reached and use it as a rallying cry to demand a reversal of our self-destructive course. I fear the consequences of overpopulation will occur so rapidly as to give little or no time for reaction. Like a deck overloaded with partygoers, all will seem fine until one too many people steps out—and then all will come crashing down before anyone knows what happened.

Our planet simply cannot support seven billion of us, not permanently anyhow. We have already had to overstretch its capacity just to support our current numbers. To feed us all, farmers have to rely on artificial fertilizers, herbicides and pesticides in order to maintain vast, unnatural monocultures euphemistically called cropland. These methods simply cannot be applied forever. Scientists know it and even most farmers know it. But instead of backpedaling, our official policy has been to declare faith that future technologies can be developed to push the envelope even farther, as if there is no limit or breaking point. That's insanity, with no vision or foresight.

What is sustainable and what is not depends on the number of people in the system. If the human population were low enough, even our current lifestyle would work for a long, long time. But it's doubtful a population that low would have enough individuals to provide the specialization of labor and competition necessary to supply our current lifestyle.

As I said, overpopulation is the biggest obstacle we face in the pursuit of sustainability. If we do not successfully reduce our numbers, nothing else we do will matter. In fact, without successfully reducing our numbers, we won't even be able to begin some of the other endeavors we will need to undertake to achieve sustainability (such as reducing the amount of food we grow).

The overpopulation problem contains elements that are both frustrating and ironic. Frustrating is the fact that it seems unlikely we will be able to willfully control our population enough to become truly sustainable. Sociologists have known for years that crowds often lack the ability to act in as reasonable a way as a single individual might when faced with a given problem. A third-person effect (it's someone else's responsibility to solve the problem) creates a tragedy of the commons, where society seems blind to a problem even while many of its constituent members are individually aware. Overpopulation is exactly one such problem. As a society, we possess the knowledge we need to solve it, but we lack the will to do so. Nature, however, is very willing to do so, and will soon step in if we don't do something first.

Biologists and ecologists still have a lot to learn about how population levels are regulated in the natural world. Charles Darwin suggested that only predation, disease, weather conditions and limits on the availability of food will keep a population of animals from increasing its population endlessly. I tend to agree with Darwin, except that I would expand the category of food to include all needed resources (food, water, habitat, etc.). I would also say competition for these resources serves as a fifth check on population growth. However, scientists know that populations of animals in closed, experimental conditions will self-regulate their numbers, without any of Darwin's checks coming into play, at a level that represents the ceiling or maximum sustainable number. Some experiments have shown that mice will stop ovulating or reproducing if the population is too large. In 1958, Silliman and Gutsell found that guppies in aquariums will keep reproducing but will cannibalize any surplus offspring when carrying capacity is reached. A study in the Nov. 23, 2000 edition of the journal Nature found that at high population levels, female arctic ground squirrels would still become pregnant, but would somehow terminate their pregnancies. How animals can gauge when their numbers have exceeded the carrying capacity and when they have been adequately reduced does not seem to be fully understood, but likely has to do with stress. It seems likely that evolution has equipped many species of animals with all the tools they need to survive, including the ability to self-regulate population levels at times of overpopulation. Presumably, this fine-tuning at the hands of evolution occurred because the species in question is more likely to survive if it self-regulates than if it relies solely on outside forces to keep its numbers in check.

The question for us is whether this finely tuned instinct for population self-regulation would manifest in human populations. Keep in mind that humans are basically domesticated animals. We have lost many of the evolutionary adaptations, both physical and instinctual, that our prehistoric ancestors needed to survive. If humans ever had an inherent ability to self-regulate population, is it still an adaptation that we possess today? Perhaps an even better question would be, "Do we want to find out?" Do we want to let our population grow so out of control that we find evidence of shunted pregnancies or cannibalism? If the evidence science has found for self-regulation in the natural world is unpalatable, perhaps we would prefer to let outside forces control our numbers. We have virtually eliminated all but one of them. There is no longer significant predation of humans to affect our numbers. Neanderthals were the last direct competition we faced as a species. Modern medicine has temporarily suppressed enough diseases and health disorders to keep them from being an effective check against overpopulation. That leaves only the inherent limitations of our planet's natural resources to provide a ceiling for human population growth. We have used technology to artificially heighten that ceiling to accommodate seven billion of us. Overstretched like a rubber band, that ceiling is now poised to snap and crash down on us, reducing the headroom to far, far below seven billion. The number of humans who would survive such a population crash remains to be seen, but population crashes usually reduce the affected species' numbers to well below the actual carrying capacity, meaning our post-crash numbers would be lower than the maximum sustainable number for the human population. Also, exceeding the carrying capacity affects the carrying capacity itself, decreasing it as renewable resources are used up faster that they can replenish themselves.

If we don't do something about human population growth, one of the aforementioned natural processes will do it for us. Humans, at least theoretically, have the intelligence to plan and act in a way that other animals can't. We are self-aware. But remember that at least once in our human history, we faced extinction because our population sank critically low. About 70,000 years ago, a supervolcano in what is now Indonesia erupted, and the resulting climate change reduced the total human population of the Earth to around 10,000 individuals. It was only a comparatively strong reproductive rate that saved us. Now we face the opposite threat of a population too large. We just have to see if our intellect can trump our biology.

What's ironic about our population dilemma is the fact that solving it requires nothing more complex than allowing attrition to naturally reduce our numbers. This could be done very quickly, very slowly, or anywhere in between. Remember that very, very few of the seven billion humans alive right now will still be alive 100 years from now. That's a powerful attrition factor. If every female who will have offspring would limit reproduction to one child, the result would be a rapid reversal of population growth. How could this be achieved? China tried it by instituting its one-child policy in 1979 and was vilified by many in the Western world, who cast the population control measure as one of the most evil manifestations of communism ever conceived. China rescinded its one-child policy in late 2015, but not because it failed. Even though the law was not a strict one-child policy and only applied to about 36 percent of the Chinese population, it was on track to stop Chinese population growth by 2030 (51 years after implementation) and actually begin shrinking the Chinese population by 2050.

News coverage of China's decision to end the controversial one-child policy was acrimonious. One particular report asserted that it was arrogant of demographers to think they could conduct population planning that would produce better results than allowing the "wisdom of the markets" to play out. By "markets," the report was referring to economic market forces, which many people believe will automatically pull population numbers in line with some optimal value, much the way supply and demand affect price. Such beliefs are disheartening and showcase the folly of mainstream thinking on this issue. If balancing human population growth is left to "the markets," famine and disease will be the tools of control. Is human misery on a planetary scale a better choice than simple reproductive restraint? Is death (through starvation, exposure, dehydration, pandemic and violence) preferable to self-control?

Because the fertility rate in "developed" nations is lower than that in "undeveloped" parts of the world, some people claim that if education and income levels everywhere can just be raised high enough, world population will settle at a sustainable level. But this wishful notion is false. Even in "developed" nations, population growth is still occurring (and even if it weren't, all of these places are already overpopulated many times over). Also, as socio-economic status goes up, so does per-capita resource friction. The richer we get, the more unsustainable our lifestyles become, so increasing socio-economic status is the solution to neither our population nor sustainability problems.

China enforced its one-child policy through penalties. Obviously, coercion is not the best way to achieve compliance with an initiative such as a one-child policy. As a society, we use laws to deter crimes such as robbery, but to make non-compliance with a population control initiative a crime would immediately set a confrontational, adversarial tone around what will already be a controversial measure. Rewarding families to do the right thing seems a better strategy. So does education and promoting social change through outreach. Education and outreach during the renaissance finally convinced Europeans that the Earth was not the center of the universe (something some astronomers had suspected for centuries but not dared to promote publicly). Education and outreach during the 1800s (along with a civil war) convinced most American that slavery was wrong. Women's rights, civil rights and gay rights are among the social movements to avail themselves of education and outreach during the 20th century. One of the most contemporary examples of promoting social change through education and outreach is the current attempt to stop bullying among school-aged children. We need to use these same strategies to inform and convince people of the catastrophe of human overpopulation. The schools and the media are the two best places to do this. Children need to hear the message incorporated across the curriculum and throughout their academic careers. And we all need the media, both news and entertainment, to weave the issue prominently throughout the messages they fill our heads with on a daily basis. Until that happens, most people will not know or care about the problem of overpopulation before it's far too late to do anything about it. It took years for network television executives and content producers to accept the fact that it was socially important to accurately represent diversity by ensuring the presence of minority characters in television programs at a rate that mirrored society. Now it's time for them to accept responsibility for ensuring an issue as important as human overpopulation is not ignored. It's no longer OK for mediated messages to pretend critical social problems do not exist.

Still, more than education and outreach are needed. Policy and regulation must be a part of the picture too. If education and outreach sufficiently raise public awareness (and affect public opinion) on the issue, then the public will support legislation because the majority will recognize that reducing overpopulation is something we must do. Most nations are not there yet, but had better figure it out in a hurry. Right now, there are at least two financial benefits to having additional children in America. That must change. First, federal income tax deductions go up with the number of dependents claimed on each form. It should be just the opposite. People (male and female) who have never parented a child should have the lightest tax burden, perhaps none at all. Once an individual has contributed to the creation of a child, he or she should pay some tax on their earnings, but the rate should be comparatively light. Once an individual has two children, he or she should pay the full prevailing tax rate but be entitled to pursue any deductions allowed by the tax code. People who have three or more children should pay a stiff tax rate and forfeit any and all deductions of any kind on all income, no matter how much they make.

Similarly, people on public assistance should not be rewarded for having more children. Under the current welfare system of IQCs (Increase for Qualified Child), payments go up as the number of dependents goes up. This too should be just the opposite. People who do not and never have had children should receive the full benefit amount. Those with one or two children (regardless of the children's ages or status as legal dependents) should receive 50 percent of the benefit. People with three or more children should be ineligible for benefits. Current taxpayers and welfare recipients should, of course, be "grandfathered" in, with the new rules applying to new applicants going forward.

The above-stated changes to the tax code and public assistance programs reverse the current system by rewarding reproductive restraint rather than activity. Still though, many would see the proposed structure as penalties levied against those who choose to have children. Another option that would escape such criticism would be to simply pay people what amounts to a bonus or rebate to keep family size small. Think of it as the Child Tax Credit in reverse—a government gratuity for helping solve our population problem. If the federal government gave individuals who remained childless an annual subsidy of $5,000 or 15 percent of their previous year's earnings, whichever is greater, nobody could accurately say anyone was being punished for having kids. Individuals with one child could receive an annual subsidy of $2,500 or 7.5 percent of their previous year's income, whichever is greater. People with two or more children would receive no bonus. The subsidy would be a bonus, received on top of whatever other income an individual received. Losing that bonus by having children would not take away one penny of anyone's earned income or cause them to pay one penny more in taxes than they otherwise would. The only people financially affected by the policy would be those who would benefit from it by not having large families.

The greatest benefit of such financial schemes to incentivize reproductive restraint would probably lie in the increased awareness and attention they would bring to the overpopulation problem. Just getting them passed into law would indicate a society willing to think in the right direction. The continuous spotlight such policies would shine on the problem would get and keep people talking about overpopulation, which we desperately need to do.

Currently, the opposition in America to either of the initiatives outlined above would be tremendous and would be launched on both fiscal and ideological grounds. But saving the human species from the catastrophic consequences of overpopulation seems to be a better use of national treasure than anything else Congress has spent money on in recent memory. That being said, solving the population problem in America, if that's even possible, would do nothing to quell world population growth. The fastest growth in world population is happening in Africa, the Middle East, southern Asia and South America. The United States, while still growing and totally unsustainable in its numbers, is not growing as quickly as the aforementioned regions. However, people in America and Europe take a much larger percapita toll on the natural resource base of the planet. An American, with his or her resource-intensive lifestyle, makes as big an impact on the planet as dozens of Africans who will never own a car or a house with central heating and air-conditioning. So while lifestyles and population growth rates vary from country to country, one fact renders all other variables irrelevant:

Human population is already too large everywhere. There are very few places where the current numbers could be maintained indefinitely. Continued growth, no matter how slow the rate, is totally out of the question.

We need to reverse human population growth, not just slow or stop it. Getting every nation of the world to agree on a plan to do that seems as close to impossible as anything I've ever heard, but that elusive agreement is the only part of the process that would be hard. If the will to exercise restraint could be found, the population problem would solve itself. Yes, we would have to figure out how to cope with shrinking in size, but if we were resourceful enough to figure out how to deal with the growing pains of expanding societies, I'm sure we would prove up to the task of managing the reversal of our numbers.

So what's a good target population number for the human species? Ridiculous are the estimates that seem to think of the Earth as a fishbowl and have the goal of seeing how many humans could be crammed into it before food and water ran out. Much more realistic are "ecological footprint" approaches that seek a balance between the Earth's productivity and the resources needed by all living things, not just humans. Clearly, we need to go back to pre-industrial population levels if we want anything approaching sustainability.

For much of our two million-year existence, and even the 200,000-year era of modern humans, our numbers were under five million worldwide. During this time, we were nomadic hunter gatherers living a subsistence lifestyle. Human population began to grow significantly when agriculture and settled existence started to replace nomadic lifestyles around 10,000 BC. By about 3,000 BC, our population topped 10 million and began an unprecedented increase. In the millennium before Christ, population grew from 50 million to about 170 million, passing the 70-million mark in about 750 BC. Our growth rate even then (adding more than 100 million people every thousand years) was itself wholly unsustainable, but if population would have leveled off then and stayed steady, it would likely have been sustainable. I say likely because no one knows for sure exactly how many people the Earth can support permanently. In fact, there is no exact number. As the carrying capacity is approached, quality of life will diminish and get steadily worse the larger the population grows. It's like filling a swimming pool with one drop of water at a time. No matter how full the pool gets, it always seems possible to add just one more drop. But spray a fire hose into an already full pool, and the evidence of overfilling will be immediate and obvious.

The carrying capacity also depends on how demanding a species is of natural resources. Our current lifestyles require far more natural resources to support than the lifestyles of those living in 750 BC. Still though, the 70-million mark is appealing. When looked at on a graph, it seems to be the point at which success for humans as a species was affirmed. We had persevered for tens of thousands of years, and at that point really showed that we had the potential of staying power. But our growth did not stop at the point of success. What had looked like the healthy, robust growth of a new species—the most successful primate species to ever inhabit the Earth—suddenly began to look like the metastatic growth of a cancer. If we would permit our numbers to drop back to where they were roughly 2,750 years ago, we would be at a wonderful place to reassess our relationship with the Earth and consider what else we might need to do to achieve sustainability. You see, the countless generations of humans and pre-human ancestors who survived ice ages, supervolcanic eruptions, desertification, fluctuations in sea level, climate change and fierce competition over the last two million years were like racers in a relay, each successfully passing the genetic baton to the next in line. They faced a gauntlet we can only imagine and ran a heroic race to bring us to where we are today. We will never know their faces or their stories, but they live within us. For us to invalidate their epic struggle by dropping that baton now because we cannot bring ourselves to correct human overpopulation would be inexcusable.

As I write this chapter in late 2012, the media are paying more attention to the concept of sustainability than ever before. But they are not taking it seriously. Just today, I heard a commentator indicate that neither the Democrat nor Republican candidate for president would dare make sustainability a part of his campaign because to get elected, politicians must promise robust and continued growth. What a sad and tragic admission. It sits at ground zero of what must change in our society.

A report this morning on the latest unemployment numbers said that 115,000 jobs created last month wasn't really a strong showing because it barely keeps up with population growth. The reference to population growth was made so matter-of-factly, it was obvious the reporter had no idea that our overpopulation problem is a far bigger story than the latest unemployment numbers. But the media have strange priorities. They will devote countless hours to stories that, like the latest unemployment numbers, will be completely irrelevant a few hundred years from now while virtually ignoring issues that will make or break the future of humanity within that same time frame.

Another report this week said the European Commission is offering a $4 million award to anyone who can find a way to make insects a protein source people will want to eat. The report indicated that such an initiative is necessary because soon, the planet will not be able to produce enough food from cows, pigs, chickens, etc. to feed all the human inhabitants. Human overpopulation or sustainability wasn't mentioned once in the report. It just accepted as legitimate the idea that instead of finding a way to reset our population at a sustainable level, we should just resort to eating bugs instead. What will humans eat when the Earth can't even produce enough bugs to feed us all? When are we going to quit grasping desperately at policies as ridiculous as transitioning humans to a diet of insects and start thinking seriously about sustainability? When are we going to quit kicking the proverbial can down the road and face our overpopulation dilemma head on?

It's easy to find models and estimates that try to predict the carrying capacity of the Earth for humans. Most of these estimates suggest a number in the billions. Some even say our planet can handle a lot more humans than are here now. One model puts the carrying capacity at 15 billion. How, given the adverse effects humans have had on the planet in just the last 200 years, anyone can suggest a number equal to or greater than our current population level would be sustainable is incomprehensible. As soon as modern man exited Africa about 90,000 years ago, the sixth great mass extinction in the history of the Earth began. Wherever humans went, accelerated extinction rates followed, and the higher our numbers got, the higher the extinction rates went. Instead of looking for population models that try to determine the maximum number of humans we can squeeze out of the Earth's resources, we need to think of the quality of life over quantity. Quality of life for humans, including the benefit of being part of a healthy, properly functioning ecosystem rich in biodiversity, is inversely proportional to our population size. That's why I believe the optimum population level for humans would be well under 100 million. I have selected 70 million as a target goal (about where we were in the year 750 BC) because if coupled with the conservation methods we know about today (such as wildlife management, sustainable agriculture and steady state economics) we could alleviate the pressure humans put on the natural resources of the planet. At 70 million, and with modern conservation know-how, we could live off the interest instead of the principal of our natural resources, and our own existence would be far less likely to negatively affect the survivability of other species.

Let's think for a moment what 70 million would mean. It is roughly one one-hundredth of our current population, meaning that there are 100 people alive today for each person alive then (seven billion divided by 100 equals 70 million). Instead of 318 million, the population of the United States would be 3.1 million (less than the current population of Connecticut but higher than that of Iowa). New York, the largest city in America, would have about 82,000 residents, significantly fewer than present day Billings, Mt., Flint, Mi., or South Bend, Ind. Alaska would have 7,200 residents, 3,000 of them in the town of Anchorage and the rest spread out over the 586,412 square miles of the state (one person for every 140 square miles). While these numbers might sound quite low, they are actually in line with the number of humans living in 750 BC in what would become the United States. Only

Embracing Sustainability

Native Americans inhabited the continent at that time, and estimates of their numbers suggest a few million people spread out across the continent in small communities. Cahokia, the most populous Native American settlement known to have existed north of Mexico, had up to 20,000 people in the 12th century. Could the 3.79 million square miles of the United States sustainably support more than 3.1 million humans? Could 1.22 square miles of average land support one human life (along with the other life already there) forever? Remember, all land in America is not rich farm country, well stocked with water and plant and animal life. There's a lot of desert, wasteland and former strip mines included. It would not be as easy as it sounds to live sustainably on that amount of land.

If you consider countries such as India, which would have 12 million of the 70 million people on Earth, things look even more questionable—much more so. India has 1.269 million square miles of land. If you do the math, that would break down to only 0.105 square miles (or 67 acres) of land per person, and that's not counting land that is under water, inhospitable like the Himalayan Mountains, or precious habitat for endangered species such as the snow leopard, Bengal tiger, Malabar civet or any of the 132 critically endangered species from India (species whose numbers are significantly below 70 million).

Reducing the human population to 1/100th of its current level may sound like something that would take many thousands of years to accomplish, but it could be done surprisingly quickly. Anyone who has ever looked into the eyes of his or her child knows that trying to tell people to have no children is not an option. But such a draconian step is not necessary. It would still be possible for every female to produce offspring, to look into the eyes of her child, and also reverse our overpopulation problem. You see, the difference between having one child and having multiple children is significant. To limit reproduction to one child is to make a great contribution to solving overpopulation. Having two children, particularly if both are boys, still puts us on track to reduce our numbers. But having three or more children or more than one girl is to be part of the problem and not part of the solution. So again, as any parent who has ever looked into the eyes of his or her child can tell you, we, the current generation, exist so that future generations may exist. It is impossible to love your children but not care about the future, because our children are who the future is for. Given our current situation (seven billion of us crowded onto a small blue planet that cannot possibly support so much human life), limiting family size to one child per couple is the best way to fulfill our obligation to those future generations. Doing so would reduce our numbers to 70 million in a mere 130 years. That's less than the length of two human lifetimes. Assuming the ratio of males to females remained close to evenly split (right now there are slightly more males than females in the world), it would at that point be necessary to increase the fertility rate to around two children per female or our numbers would continue to shrink below desirable levels.

The realization that we are so tantalizingly close (130 years) to bringing our population level under control should be so exciting as to inspire us to act. Overpopulation is the single biggest threat to our continued survival as a species, but we could vanquish that threat in a little more than a century if we chose to do so. That means that many of the people living at the moment the problem was solved would have personally known people who were alive when the quest to solve it was begun. Willfully solving our own overpopulation problem would be the single greatest achievement in human history, not because of the complexity of the task or the brainpower necessary to solve it, but because of the importance it would hold for our future and for what it would say about our character and our priorities. The key to our salvation is right in front of us. Will we take it?

Sadly, the answer to that question is probably no, at least not unless human thinking and behavior change markedly in a short period of time. Education is a powerful way to change thinking and behavior. Maybe in this age of globalization and massification through the internet and social media, we are closer to the capacity for rapid evolution in human thinking and behavior than we realize. But for now, even though the solution to our overpopulation problem is as simple as reducing the fertility rate to one child per female, the likelihood of achieving consensus among every nation on Earth—the world's entire human population—seems completely impossible, especially considering there's very little time left to achieve such a diplomatic miracle before the catastrophic results of overpopulation become inescapable.

Accepting this sad reality, the pragmatic question becomes whether it is possible to have a population "island" or "islands," a place or places on earth where the population is below the carrying capacity and all aspects of human existence are managed to be sustainable. It's unclear whether it would be possible to maintain these pockets of sustainability while the human population in other parts of the world experienced crashes or regional extinctions resulting from overpopulation.

Diseases we could not control might, depending on their vectors, spread from overpopulated regions to the sustainably populated areas adjacent to them. Also, climate change and changes to global ecosystems could make it harder for humans to survive, even in areas outside of the overpopulated regions that gave rise to those changes. For instance, droughts, floods and abnormal variations in seasonal temperatures would not respect political or geographical boundaries. And if human overpopulation affects biodiversity and regional ecosystems in the wrong ways, the result could be the loss of beneficial species that help humans survive, such as pollinating insects, or a big increase in invasive or indigenous species that could make human existence harder. The web of life on Earth is intertwined in ways we don't fully understand, so it is not at all a safe assumption that human-induced disruptions to natural systems in one area would remain in that area, allowing pockets of sustainable populations to remain insulated from the chaos erupting in other parts of the world.

2) Per-capita Consumption of Natural Resources

Next to being too numerous, our second biggest unsustainable attribute would be how high-maintenance most humans are, especially in developed nations. Humans consume natural resources at a shocking rate. Some of these resources are non-renewable or finite in nature. I'm speaking primarily of fossil fuels. We shouldn't be using these anyhow, for reasons I'll discuss elsewhere, but basing our existence on something we know will run out is crazy. How can any rational person support such a policy? In addition to fueling our industry and daily lives with these finite fossil fuel resources, we make most of our clothing, our roads and parking lots, a sizable portion of our household items and even our homes themselves out of them. Life as we know it without hydrocarbons would be unimaginable, and that's a problem because within a few generations, our traditional source of these chemicals will dry up. Synthesizing them artificially is neither practical nor sustainable. Relying on resources that are not both naturally occurring and renewable just doesn't make good sense, especially if the production and use of those unnatural resources carries hidden costs.

One might think the news would be better regarding the renewable natural resources we use, but it is not. We are currently consuming many of these at such high rates that they are effectively finite as well. Although they are renewable, we are using them faster than they can replenish themselves, and so they too are running out.

Aldo Leopold was among the first to tell us that it is unwise to engage in ecological practices that run counter to the natural order of things. Monocultures are rare in nature. Even the boreal forests of the far North, which seem to lack much diversity, are home to a healthy balance of life forms that both compete with and complement each other in some surprising ways. A corn or wheat field in Iowa is not at all the same thing. It is a violation of the laws of biodiversity. We have had to use unnatural, artificially contrived chemicals just to bootstrap these vast monocultures into existence. We harvest them relentlessly every year and then replant, again relying on our artificial and temporary alterations to create a set of conditions that allow this aberration. Without it, we could not possibly feed ourselves. We are banking our existence on an untenable experiment in unsustainable agriculture, all to feed seven billion people. The topsoil is already functionally depleted and could not possibly produce the volume of crops it currently does without artificial fertilizers, the runoff of which is now beginning to pollute our waterways and cause toxic algae blooms. Pesticides, herbicides and genetic modification have temporarily kept us one step ahead of the inevitable assault nature will wage against our monoculture croplands. A monoculture is a vacuum, and nature will never allow it to stand. It is an irresistible force.

Equally as bad as the unsustainable way we produce our food are the method and rate with which we create all the other stuff we spend our lives collecting. As Madonna said 30 years ago, we are living in a material world. It seems impossible for us to resist amassing stuff. Some people on Earth can pack all their worldly possessions on their backs, but for those of us in "developed" nations, that notion is hopelessly impossible. Even people who consider themselves minimalists and who abhor cluttered basements, attics and garages could never hope to limit their holdings to an amount that could be carried simultaneously by anything but a large truck. It doesn't help that a large and effective marketing force has permeated our culture with the message that to be happy, we must consume. It might not be so bad if all these material goods lasted long enough to span several generations, but very little of it does. In fact, anything that lasts even a single human lifetime is considered an heirloom, interesting if for no other reason than its longevity. Most of the stuff we pack home from Wal-Mart and similar retailers is destined to be discarded for various reasons within a few years at most. Very little of this stuff is designed so that its production and use will be sustainable. Instead, it is made to appeal to our desire to possess stuff that we believe will be useful and/or fun. Perhaps this longing for material satisfaction is more instinct than desire. Early humans benefited mightily from effective tools and other useful items. Coveting them may have been crucial for survival. But that same instinct manifesting in today's consumer world is an unsustainable recipe for disaster. It has turned even the resource-conscious among us into slaves of our possessions.

If there's one word that really fits our consumeristic ways, it's "excess." We produce "stuff" in excess of what the Earth can sustainably provide. It's produced in quantities that exceed our needs. It is packaged in a way that is greatly in excess of what is really necessary. Excessive resources and energy are wasted transporting this stuff to every corner of the world. The stores that it's sold in are excessive in their size, excessive in the resources used to construct them, excessive in the energy they burn to create a store atmosphere that will maximize sales, and excessive in the waste they create. It's the Earth that pays the price for all this excess—excess that exists because sustainability is not a priority for the people selling all this stuff or for the people buying it.

3) Production of Waste and Pollution

As bad as our materialistic ways is the fact that throughout our lifetimes, we throw away much more than we keep and produce pollution on a ridiculous scale. As discussed elsewhere, most people produce tons of household waste every year and unceremoniously ship it off to a landfill, even though virtually all of it could be either composted, recycled or incinerated. But adding to the tragedy of this is the fact that manufacturing all the stuff that ends up in our garbage also includes the production of waste. Talk about double jeopardy, waste and pollution are produced in the process of making stuff that ends up as waste and pollution. Most of our daily lives are spent at activities that directly or indirectly contribute to a waste stream that has, in just a matter of decades, overwhelmed the Earth's ability to absorb and detoxify as it does for the waste produced by all other living things. Ours is the only waste that is poisoning the air, water and soil almost everywhere around the globe. No other animal is guilty of this crime.

Production of waste and pollution is by far the easiest of the top three obstacles to sustainability to solve. Renewables are a robust answer to fossil fuels, which account for most of our air pollution. If we focused on efficiency and reduced our energy usage to only what is really necessary, renewables could sustain us. Fossil fuels definitely cannot.

Our solid waste/landfill problem is also about as easy to fix as any of the obstacles standing between us and sustainability. With a bit of tweaking on the part of industry to make sure nothing is produced and sold that doesn't fit the model of recycle/compost/incinerate, we could become a zero-landfill society where there's no need for anything to ever be "thrown away."

Unfortunately, we have instead become a throwaway society—both in practice and in spirit. Not only do we consume and discard material items at a quantity and rate that is inefficient, unnecessary and unsustainable, we have adopted a worldview that accepts this wanton waste as normal. We are not ashamed at all of our landfills. There is no guilt in filling a garbage bag with junk and tossing it in a dumpster. This shameless acceptance of waste extends to our attitude regarding the planet. We don't even think about conservation, efficiency or sustainability. The notions of using as little as possible and leaving nothing but tracks are familiar to conservation-minded folks, but are conspicuously absent from the population at large, our industries and government. Until sustainability becomes a fixture within those institutions, we will not solve this or any of our problems, and if we don't solve our problems, we will perish.

Landfills and Human Shame

Have you ever seen a caged animal living in such horrid conditions that it was forced to sit, stand or lie in its own excrement? Fortunately such a sight is rare, but when it happens, the animal at first tries to avoid the filth as best as it can. But when conditions no longer permit that, it resigns itself to the inevitable. It is impossible to look at a working landfill and not see the same image. We humans, prisoners of our own consumptive lifestyle and throwaway culture, are soiling our own bed, and the sight is a pathetic one. We defile vast areas with our waste, piling it up day after day until that spot can hold no more. Then we cover it up with dirt and move on to the next "sanitary landfill." Such a euphemism pretends that the result is something other than what it is.

All life depends on a clean, properly functioning planet. It is not sustainable to turn parts of that planet into wastelands of foul, toxic garbage. Every acre of landfill we create has the effect of reducing the size of the earth by the same amount because that land no longer functions as it should. It is not an acre from which the water can be drunk or the soil used to produce food. It is no longer an acre of habitat capable of supporting a healthy ecosystem. It is now a ticking time bomb waiting to inevitably mix its toxic contents with the air, land and water that makes up the rest of our planet. How long can we do this to the Earth? When will the inevitable pushback begin?

Our puny efforts to contain and manage the landfills can only be maintained as long as we as a society have the resources to do so. Geologic time will take whatever we put into the ground and mix it with the air, soil and water everywhere. Nothing is forever in nature. The land mass that is now Antarctica was at one time a tropical rain forest. The highest points of the Himalayan Mountains were at one time the flat bottom of an ancient ocean. The Great Lakes are but infants of geologic time, the result of mile-thick glaciers scouring out hundreds of feet of dirt and rock during the last ice age as easily as a child digs in a sand box. How can anyone who understands the churning and turning of the Earth's crust think a plastic sheet and a leachate treatment system operated by humans and regulated by some government agency can protect the Earth—forever—from the legacy of toxic filth we are creating for ourselves?

The Earth is a closed system, and we are filling it with waste that will not go away. Disposing of it in landfills is a process that will collapse if continued to the breaking point. Will we stop when 1 percent of the Earth's surface is landfill? Will we try for 5 percent or 10 percent? Will we wait until there's not enough untainted land left to sustain life or until we lose control of the process and toxicity from the defiled areas spreads outward?

Embracing Sustainability

People who accumulate filth in their houses will eventually succumb to the health effects, be evicted or have the property condemned as unfit for human habitation. We've all read the news stories of some demented person found living in a house with garbage and other filth piled knee deep. Usually there's a picture or description of authorities donning haz-mat suits and gas masks just to walk in the place. Most of us think there's something mentally wrong with someone who allows filth to fill the living space of his or her home. But as a society, we are doing this very thing to the one home we cannot just raze and rebuild—our home planet. The only thing scarier than the fact that our elected officials say it's OK to defile the Earth with filth is the fact that most people do so without a second thought.

Until we transform ourselves into a zero landfill society, we will remain as pathetic and deserving of pity as a caged animal lying in its own excrement. Is that how you want to be perceived or remembered? The solution is very much within our reach. As a society, we need to regulate industry so that nothing that cannot be recycled infinitely, composted or incinerated without toxic residue is allowed to be manufactured. With rare exceptions for certain limited applications, plastic should be banned. In the rare instances when plastic is used, it must be made from sustainably grown plant-based oil and must be destroyed at the end of its useful life so that it cannot enter the biosphere of our planet. We need to implement comprehensive waste management programs in which all refuse is collected and taken to sorting facilities where recyclable and compostable materials are separated and dealt with accordingly and items that require incineration to neutralize are completely destroyed. Under such a system, we as a society would have to accept a somewhat less convenient lifestyle and pay more to manage our waste stream, but the result—sustainability—would be a bargain by any measure.

Pride in Our Species

Are we proud of our species? There are, at best count, 196 different flags representing the nations of the world. But there is not one that flies in honor of humanity as a whole. Why do we never celebrate who we really are?—Homo sapiens. We have, after all, achieved quite a few remarkable distinctions that no other life form in our planet's history has ever approached. We have unparalleled intelligence, and while other species are amazing in their abilities to adapt to the sometimes harsh conditions of life on Earth, we are unmatched in our ability to manipulate the world around us to suit our needs. It remains to be seen if our accomplishments along these lines can last or whether our species is a proverbial flash in the pan, a brilliant spark of great but short-lived success. Avoiding such a depressing end lies, to a great extent, in how we carry ourselves.

So are we? Are we proud of our species? 1) Are we thankful for what our ancestors have done for us? 2) Do we conduct ourselves in a way that ensures future generations can look back at our age with gratitude? 3) Do we even respect ourselves, those living in the current?

Unfortunately, the answer to those questions is no. We are not thankful for, but rather are forced to endure and try to correct, the actions of our recent ancestors. With the exception of bodies of work in science, medicine, the arts and literature, much of what was done before our time were self-serving indulgences meant only to provide instant gratification to those alive at the time. Gone are the days of bending down to take a drink of clean, pure water from the average river or stream. Even a lot of spring water is now unsafe. There's not a place on the planet, even in the remote arctic, where pollution put into the air decades ago cannot be found. The middle of the Pacific Ocean is home to a floating mess of garbage, much of it plastic, the size of a continent. Acid rain, heavy metals and unnatural chemicals most of us know nothing about have made their way up through every food chain on the planet. Even our climate has been markedly impacted by the choices and thoughtless actions of past generations. Instead of trying to fix the problems, we argue and fight and use these issues as another excuse to divide ourselves and hate one another. Our ancestor's insatiable compulsion to destroy the natural world in pursuit of personal gain once had a name—manifest destiny. Now it seems as if it's our destiny to perpetuate their misdeeds.

As for our conduct, the answer is again no. Very few of us think of the future or our progeny. There is no precedent for that type of thinking. We have no history of caring about sustainability.

And not only don't we care about the future, we for the most part don't even care about conserving the natural resources we need right now for our current existence. Why does it have to be this way, and what can we do to change those three answers to "yes"?

Our intelligence, a product of evolution, has given us the chance to live in unprecedented comfort. But the lifestyle it has led us to has made us vulnerable. We are perhaps the least flexible species currently in existence. Any shift or disruption in our artificial life support system (built environment) threatens our survivability. To improve our situation, we need to develop some "fandom" or "patriotism" about our own species and its future. About the only enthusiasm I see for our species is an arrogant sense of superiority over other life. We test drugs and conduct experiments on animals because we don't see them as equal in value to human life. Such a tendency is about the only evidence of pride in ourselves as a species. Religious doctrine contains even more arrogant assertions that all of creation was put here for our exclusive use and benefit. That dangerously selfish notion actually works against the approach I'm promoting—to cultivate some positive enthusiasm for our species and work to ensure our survival. We need to strive for sustainability if we wish to remain a fixture on this Earth. Evolution has programmed all life to scream out for survival. Passing along one's genes and ensuring the survival of the next generation are hardwired into every living thing. We are no exception, but we seem unable or unwilling to recognize what really needs to happen to promote our own survival.

The world over, I see more enthusiasm for sports teams, religions and countries or nation states than I do for ourselves as a species. Why aren't we eager to develop and embrace practices and positions that would maximize our chances of survival as a species? Instead, we jeopardize that survival in exchange for instant gratification, short-term gain and personal comfort. Evolutionarily, these are maladaptive characteristics. Imagine if instead of being filled with hatred and warfare, the world was united in the pursuit of sustainable practices that would ensure the long-term survival of the human species.

There has been a lot of talk in recent years (in both the movies and the science community) about protecting the Earth from asteroid strikes. The notion of deflecting an asteroid that's on a collision course with Earth seems an odd priority given that such a threat occurs at intervals of millions of years. When is the last time our policies or initiatives have reflected a vision millions of years into the future? We seem unable to muster concern for even the next hundred years when it comes to our use of plastics and fossil fuels, but suddenly we want to protect ourselves from an asteroid strike? Wouldn't it be great if we showed such concern and willingness to act on all issues that threaten our future?

Imagine if we took pride in finding ways to make the smallest possible impact on the planet—to leave it, for the next generation, in even better shape than we found it—to strive for maximum sustainability. Imagine if all the nations of the world came together to pursue sustainability for our species and if the only competition or struggle between nations was to see which one could make the greatest contribution toward that end? Such a goal is so far removed from our current priorities as to boggle the mind. It's sobering to see, in a moment of clairvoyance, how flawed our current lifestyle is. We are said to be the only species that is self aware, the only species capable of pondering our own destiny. Why then, won't we do so? Why don't we care that our lifestyle is wholly untenable?

When it comes to issues of medicine and public health, we confront every threat from the biggest to the smallest. There are huge efforts under way to cure cancer, AIDS, Alzheimer's, Parkinson's and many other diseases. Flu shots are readily available everywhere. Immunizations are required for children to attend school. We focus heavily on these medical and health issues, and we don't hesitate to enact laws necessary to facilitate our progress (just investigate how many aspects of our lives public health departments are legally entitled to regulate). But when it comes to the threats of an unsustainable lifestyle, few people want to find and enact solutions. What if it became trendy for everyone from individuals to governments and humanity as a whole to tweak every aspect of our existence, from the biggest to the smallest, to maximize sustainability?

There's a tangible satisfaction that comes from having a freezer full of organic meat and vegetables harvested from the land around one's home. There's a real sense of comfort in knowing a winter's worth of firewood is cut, split and stacked in a convenient spot. These personal pleasures are derived from only one year's worth of good planning on the part of one individual. Imagine how comforting it would be to know that our species was on a truly sustainable tract that would ensure our long-term survival? To know that our children, grandchildren and all future generations were guaranteed a healthy and fruitful existence because of our good planning would be the ultimate comfortable notion. As it stands, we are burdened with the opposite reality. Because we paid absolutely no attention to sustainability when constructing our society, we are vexed by the realization that our progeny have a dim, short-lived future. I believe more people are aware of this sad fact than most people might expect. Deep down, even people who would deny it have an awareness that as a society, we are very sick. These people may be unable to articulate the specific problem or even identify in general terms where we are going wrong, but they sense that all is not well.

I believe this awareness that society is unsustainable in its current state wears on the subconscious of many people and is the root of much of the moral decay we see in our culture today. I've long since lost count of the number of conversations I've had with people in which they lamented a decline or decay in society. "We never used to have to lock our doors, and we could let our kids play outside all day without worrying," they say. "But things are different now. Times have changed and not for the better. I really worry about what it will be like for the next generation. I'm kind of glad I won't be around to see it." Such fears are on the minds of many people. But why are things different today? What has changed in our society? I believe one of the biggest changes is an increased awareness (or subconscious sense) that our current lifestyles are unsustainable. It's like a great taboo that everyone feels but no one dares to speak about. Who wants to be burdened with the knowledge that his or her entire existence is so fatally flawed that it cannot be maintained for more than another generation or two before the dysfunctional aspects of it become so problematic that the entire system collapses under its own weight? Talk about being part of the problem instead of part of the solution. No sane person would be happy knowing this. No wonder so many people respond to environmental rhetoric by saying, "What do I care? I'll be dead by the time all these bad things happen." They, of course, don't really mean it, but it's the only way they know to cope with a problem that otherwise seems overwhelming to them. Outright denial is another coping mechanism. Apathy is the third and perhaps most common way of coping with the dissonance of knowing our society is unsustainable. A majority, it seems, just lose themselves in the machinations of their daily lives and allow themselves to be blinded to the truth by their choice to attend only to the banal and meaningless.

But all this apathy and dissonance have a cost. Frankly put, when people don't give a damn, it shows. That is, I believe, what is happening in society today. It's what is behind the change in society so many people lament these days. When people believe the game is lost, that there is no hope for the future, they will quit caring about the things they should. The phenomenon reminds me of how morale in a beehive can change. In a healthy hive that is strong and surviving well (sustainable), the bees are happy and productive. But in a doomed hive—one with a poor queen, no queen at all, inadequate food supplies or disease—the bees are either irritable and aggressive or morose. They know, somehow, that their colony is collapsing, and they respond with unhealthy, antisocial behavior. So it is with our society. The daily news reports are full of the proof. They are chronicling the evidence of a society in a downward spiral. People, of course, notice. But instead of springing into action to make things right, most people ignore the problems and attend only to trivial distractions—sports, celebrity/entertainment news, sensationalism, or even "news" about issues of little significance (such as the almost constant coverage of politics and government, even though these institutions are doing almost nothing to solve the most important problems we face). Ironically, it's the people who display normal, healthy reactions to the dire problems we face that are labeled weird or unbalanced by "mainstream" society. "Radical" protesters who lie down in front of bulldozers or chain themselves to the steps of the state legislature in an attempt to raise awareness and change unsustainable policies are viewed with skepticism at best or disdain at worst. But they are heroes, not weirdos.

We are drawn irresistibly to technology. As a species, technology has been our hallmark since we split from a dozen or more hominid lines and began our rise to power 200,000 years ago. Technology is what has enabled us to be what we are. It is who we are. For all of recorded history, and definitely today, the latest technology is the definition of cool. Having the latest technology is an understood must (or at least an implied benefit) in our culture. But what have generations of technological triumph netted us besides a cushy but unsustainable lifestyle? Our technological pursuits have been only for purposes of personal pleasure, profit, war, or the enablement of additional unsustainable practices. So very little of our technological muscle has been put toward the one thing it should: ensuring our survival, finding ways of living sustainably. Renewable energy should have and could have replaced fossil fuels by the end of World War II. But the only true progress that remains for humans to achieve—progress toward sustainability—has been stalled by lies about feasibility, cost and jobs. If we would focus our efforts and our technology on survival and sustainability, we might just achieve it. And if we would apply the same zeal toward sustainability as we do to religion, sports, politics, patriotism and instant gratification, we would be healthier. If we were enthused and motivated to achieve sustainability—if we viewed it as the foundational virtue of our individual and collective lives instead of a buzzword to maybe pay some lip service to (as long as said lip service wasn't too serious and didn't interfere with the status quo), we might just make it as a species.

As a culture, we prize a strong work ethic. We seem to agree that doing our job right, no matter what that job is, is a quality to be valued and respected. Why then, don't we value doing right by the most important job facing humanity? If we took pride, real pride, in achieving sustainability and ensuring our survival, we would feel enormously better about ourselves and would be an infinitely healthier and better adjusted species. No more denial. No more dissonance. No more apathy. Instead we would be a vivacious culture with a proud heritage of caring and planning for the lives of unborn generations, and each generation would be overflowing with a gracious eagerness to do even better, to build on the loving gift left by their ancestors and to pass the torch of sustainability into an unknown but secure future.

Dual Perspectives—Evolution and Conservation

A sizable percentage of Americans do not "believe" in evolution. The scientific community, however, is unanimous in its acceptance of the idea that life on Earth is constantly being fine-tuned as random mutations face the test of natural selection. The concept is so completely logical that one does not need to be a geneticist to grasp it. Nor does it take a genius to comprehend the elegance of the process responsible for the amazing clockwork of nature. All that is required to recognize the validity of biological evolution is a very minimal appreciation of the natural world. I use the word appreciation in the same way the humanities community uses it to describe art appreciation or music appreciation. In this application, appreciation does not mean thankfulness but rather an awareness or comprehension of main qualities or characteristics. It seems that many people lack this appreciation for nature. They have almost no ability to comprehend even the most basic mechanisms of the natural world. It's as if their minds are wired in such a way as to prevent an understanding of anything to do with nature. Nature is a foreign and unrecognizable concept for them.

I have known people who seem utterly unable to grasp mathematics—even on a basic level. I have also known people with almost no ability to express themselves in writing. I've known people who say they are unable to cook, sew, sing, dance, read a map, repair mechanical devices or understand the metric system. I believe some of these claims of ineptitude are legitimate, particularly in the areas of music, athletics, math or writing. But in other cases, part—sometimes a large part—of the disconnect seems to be attitudinal. Some people don't want to engage certain content areas or pursuits. The reasons may be many. Lack of interest, fear of failure, the perception that the reward doesn't seem worth the effort needed to achieve it all explain why we sometimes put up walls between ourselves and certain experiences. So does our self identity. We spend our lives defining ourselves—figuring out who we are and who we aren't, what we stand for and what we don't. And once we have a blueprint of ourselves mapped out, we tend to avoid anything that would conflict with it. This is not to say that people don't have eclectic tastes. Many do. But no matter how pluralistic the set of topics someone may embrace, an area that is anathema to their self identity will be rejected.

So it is with people who cannot comprehend nature. Part of it may be that they legitimately have no frame of reference for it. If they were raised in a way that made them strangers to the natural world, they will not understand nature. But a greater part, I believe, is that they have defined themselves in a way that they believe to be incompatible with an appreciation of the natural world. Rush Limbaugh, for instance, may tell his listeners that he had a great day playing golf. But his appreciation of the day would probably not include having seen the morning dew sparkling on thousands of spider webs in the rough, or a killdeer defending its ill-placed nest at the edge of a sand trap, the sound of cicadas or the way a crisp north breeze seemed to instantly rattle every leaf on an aspen tree beside the fairway. To even mention such things would immediately alienate much of Limbaugh's audience, who like him, have probably defined themselves in a way that specifically precludes appreciation or even notice of the natural world. To such people, nature's only consequence would be the extent to which it factored into the golf game. Fair weather may be appreciated if it made the game more enjoyable. But it would not be seen as a beautiful reminder of our planet's temperate and life-giving climate. An imposing water hazard's only worth would be the challenge it added to the 14th hole, not its role as wetland habitat. The golf course itself would be seen as universally positive—a useful "development" of "vacant land." Never would a moment be spent pondering whether the alteration of the land to build the golf course increased the diversity of habitat in the area or merely served as additional loss of habitat of a higher value than what was created.

The differences between the way Limbaugh would and would not appreciate a day of golf have, I believe, more to do with the way he has defined himself—the parameters he has set for what he will accept and what he will reject—than anything else. And so it is with the nearly half of Americans who refuse to accept evolution as the explanation for the amazing variety of life on Earth. To profess acceptance of the concept would be to admit that they had thought about and understood nature—and that is, simply put, not something some people will ever allow themselves to do. You see, evolution is part of nature. It is a function of the natural world. Accepting the concept of evolution would require one to admit that something to do with nature is valid and amazing and of great value. Making such an admission is also something some people would never do. I can't find any poll data on the subject, but I suspect there is a strong correlation between being concerned about conservation issues and accepting the theory of biological evolution. Both require a base appreciation of the natural world. People who have that appreciation of nature seem likely both to care about our species' impact on the planet and to see the brilliant simplicity of how evolution drives life on Earth. To people with the appreciation, both are "no brainers." But to people without that appreciation of nature—to whom nature is a foreign and unfamiliar realm from which they desire to distance themselves—neither evolution nor conservation makes any sense whatsoever.

The seeming desire of some to distance themselves from nature reveals itself in another dimension of the divide over evolution. Those who accept evolution see it as a magnificent explanation of how all life came to be what it is today. But those who reject it fixate on its application to humans. They seem to be deeply troubled by the idea that modern humans evolved from apes. Their biggest hang-up seems to be that they believe apes are "animals" (and thus part of nature) while humans are not "animals" and have always been separate from nature. To suggest that we are part of the same teeming caldron of life as the rest of the plants and animals on Earth is abhorrent to them and serves as their main objection to evolution. If Darwin had suggested evolution only explained how tortoises and finches came to possess their current forms, many of the same people who reject his theory may not pay it much mind. But because it places humans on the same stage as the rest of life on Earth—that stage being nature—they can't stand the idea.

    This lack of appreciation, almost disdain, of nature extends to conservation issues as well. Those who dismiss conservation as tree huggers' nonsense seem to believe that nature is dirty, menacing, worthless unless somehow monetized, unworthy of respect, devoid of any rights, and both inferior to and unrelated to human existence. Various studies suggest acceptance of evolution and concern for conservation issues are both correlated with education, meaning the more highly educated, the more likely one is to both accept the concept of evolution and support conservation. Although I can't find any poll data on the subject, I bet the two are more strongly correlated with each other than either is with education. There is just too much connecting these dual perspectives in the universe of public opinion. Understanding how and why they are similar is a revealing look into the mindset of those who just can't seem to grasp the bigger picture of life on Earth.

Embracing Sustainability

Wisdom versus Waste

    Being that I try to remain optimistic about things whenever possible, I would like to think there's hope that we humans can right our foolish ways before it's too late for us. At times, I feel we just might. But other times, I witness something that convinces me we're utterly doomed. That's exactly how I felt yesterday when I saw a New York Times article announcing "Race is on as Ice Melt Reveals Arctic Treasures." (Page A1, Sept. 19, 2012). With a dateline of Nuuk, Greenland, the lead paragraph proclaimed, "With Arctic ice melting at a record pace, the world's superpowers are increasingly jockeying for political influence and economic position in outposts like this one, previously regarded as wastelands." The second paragraph continues, "At stake are the Arctic's abundant supplies of oil, gas and minerals that are, thanks to climate change, becoming newly accessible along with increasingly navigable polar shipping shortcuts."

    I used to think that as the consequences of our meddling with the clockwork of the planet became incontrovertible, we would display some wisdom and change course. But if the New York Times article is any indication, we are not likely to do so. Even as our use of fossil fuels erases the arctic as we know it, we see only new opportunities to get even more fossil fuels that had previously been locked out of reach by the ice. We are truly a ship of fools, no more capable of self-control than any other animal on this planet. When our impact becomes too great, we will experience a massive setback—a rebalancing—dealt to us by mother nature. It's painful to be a passenger on that ship of fools—prescient enough to see our misguided policies as the mistakes they are but powerless to grab the wheel and right our course.

    I've brought two beautiful children into this world. I love them more than anything and would gladly give my own life to make theirs better. I exist so that they may exist. But I am forced to watch their future—the world that must be right if it is to support their children and children's children—be compromised and abused beyond repair. That makes me mad as hell. What gives the elites of society—heads of state and leaders of industry—the right to hurt my children by wrecking their future? And why do my objections fall on deaf ears? Those among us who hold the most power—the power of authority, the power of influence—have an ethical responsibility to do what's right, not stand idly by while my children's future is harmed.

    If I were president, or a congressman, or a federal judge, or a billionaire, or a media mogul, I could do much more than I can now to effect a positive change in the direction of society. I could do more than I can now to protect the future of my children. Why does it seem my moral conviction is a scarce one, especially among powerful individuals? Why are they satisfied with the status quo while I am not? Perhaps they are satisfied because it is the status quo that has made them who they are. I do not know. I know only that it is incredibly frustrating to see the error but be powerless to make enough of a change to fix what's wrong.

Are our current lifestyle and behavior the result of giving a hominid species enough intelligence to achieve an industrial revolution? Perhaps apes were not the best recipient for that intelligence. What if a species with reptilian ancestry had been the first to use tools and technology to advance? Perhaps it's our endothermic bias, but reptiles seem too cold to be conscientious executors of that power. What about a species of bird? Mastering flight was a great accomplishment and showed great potential for adaptability. But that adaptability never embraced higher intelligence. Perhaps birds, with their enviable gift of flight and, in many cases, great beauty, would have grown even more narcissistic and self-centered than humans if given intelligence and self-awareness. Perhaps a mammal other than ourselves would have handled great intelligence better than we did. Whales and elephants are already credited with higher than average intelligence within the animal kingdom, but whether by land or sea, size seems to have been the key to success for these species. To my mind, bears are as likely a candidate as any to handle great intelligence well. Despite being large, incredibly strong and armed with deadly teeth and claws, they are generally shy and do little unnecessary harm. Most people, if endowed with their physical gifts, would proclaim themselves the toughest things around and go out looking for every fight they could find. But bears seldom show such unprovoked mean-spiritedness. Although they could kill any creature in the woods, they prefer to walk away from a fight when possible and kill only what they need—not one thing more. Yes, bears can be very dangerous, but anyone who really understands their nature would probably admit they would have done at least as good a job as us, perhaps better, if given our station.

Ironically, in many ways some of the least intelligent creatures on Earth have shown the greatest ability to self-regulate in the interest of sustainability. Honeybees "know" what must be done to survive another year. Although their actions are purely instinctual and never the result of conscious decision-making, honeybees do what must be done to ensure their colony's survival. In early spring, the number of bees in the colony swells greatly, and summer is spent making enough honey to carry the colony through winter. Bees do this even though most of the workers who toil throughout summer will not be alive to partake of the harvest during winter. They do what the must—selflessly—to ensure the future. They achieve sustainability. And when fall comes to an end, most of the workers who are still alive leave the honey-laden hive and die alone of starvation so that the youngest can survive to do it all again next year. How does our concern for the future compare

Embracing Sustainability

with that of the lowly honeybee? Before answering, keep in mind that we are by far the most intelligent species on Earth and pride ourselves on an ability to comprehend and solve big problems! So how are we doing? How is the most intelligent species on Earth—the self-appointed steward of the planet—doing at ensuring it remains the elegant cradle of life we first glimpsed through human eyes 200,000 years ago? The answer is, obviously, not well at all. Our behavior on this planet has been absolutely abhorrent for the last 500 years or so. We have run amuck like hooligans trashing the place—thugs on a vandalism spree. We ought to be ashamed, but instead we are arrogant. We tell ourselves that God put everything on this planet for our exclusive use and benefit. We ignore the fact that even if that were true, our current practices are ruining it for everyone who will come after us. That surely is not what God intended.

There is a scene in the 1996 movie "Independence Day" in which one of the alien invaders is captured and taken to the secret "Area 51" where our government allegedly hides evidence of extraterrestrial visitors to our planet. The aliens in this movie are, of course, portrayed as highly intelligent, with technology far beyond our own. The president of the United States enters Area 51 to see the captured alien. Despite being sequestered behind a glass wall, the creature seems to immediately know which of the humans staring at it is the highest in authority. It telepathically channels into the mind of the president, who asks if there can be peace between us and them. The alien hisses "no peace." The president then asks, as diplomatically as he can, what the aliens want us to do. In an evil voice, the alien says "die" and them telepathically attacks the president, exerting some sort of lethal force into the commander in chief's brain. A secret service agent shoots out the glass and then guns down the hissing, flailing alien, freeing the president from its telepathic grip just in time. After catching his breath, the president says that during the period of mental connectivity, he was able to see into the mind of the alien and witness what the invaders planned for the Earth. He declares that they are like locusts that move from planet to planet, using up every natural resource before leaving a wasted and worthless world behind. The grim visage steels the resolve of the president, who then helps an unlikely band of human fighters to defeat the alien invaders.

The subtext is clear: The invaders in the movie have no compassion, no soul, no mercy. Humans, by comparison, have humanity. That virtuous humanity, coupled with an unbeatable will to survive, ensures that we, the good guys, come out the winner. We humans will ensure a long, bright future for ourselves and our planet, both of which the aliens were about to destroy.

Unfortunately, that sentiment is just a feel-good movie moment. The truth is, we are much more like the aliens of "Independence Day" than most of us would care to admit. Ask any other species on Earth, from passenger pigeons to polar bears, how much humanity, how much compassion, how much mercy we show for the life of this planet. Ask them how much we care about anything but ourselves and our own selfish pursuits. To them, we are those invaders without souls who stand ready to exterminate anything standing between us and our desire to use up every natural resource the Earth has to offer. "Race is on as Ice Melt Reveals Arctic Treasures." Indeed.

The Peace of Loneliness

Do you ever feel as if the Earth just isn't big enough? If you live in the cramped suburbs that sprawl across the Eastern United States, you might long for true wilderness, a place where one could walk for days and find nothing but an unspoiled wild horizon as vast as the sea. As a child, I used to believe the woods around my parent's house were that type of limitless wild kingdom. Even as I became aware that they really were not, I managed to find a way to feel as if they were while hiking or hunting in them. It wasn't until I became older, in my 30s and 40s, that the relentless march of subdivisions and urban sprawl began to eat away at the magic in my soul as it had been doing to the countryside for decades. Like termite damage to a board, the destruction of my childhood stomping grounds finally became severe enough to dampen (but not extinguish) the fire I had kindled in my heart for what once seemed like a woodland paradise.

It is still possible to find a secluded spot in those hills and tuck oneself away in the cradling arms of the woods and pretend—pretend to have slipped into some remote corner that time forgot. For that moment, everything manmade is gone. Nothing exists for a thousand miles except countless hilltops, each warmed by the same sunrise, caressed by the same west wind and separated only by one pristine hollow after another—a landscape of which each acre, each foot, each inch is unique in the way the elements of life are arranged thereon and yet branded as kin, stamped with a sameness that defines an ecoregion as home to a richly diverse but fixed set of plant and animal life. Oh to be immersed in such a place. For that moment, the feeling is of being rooted to the spot as firmly as any tree and yet also free to drift like a spirit to every ridgetop or any sheltered corner of this unending paradise. But the illusion cannot last, for paradise has been shattered and exists only in the mind's eye.

Even the Eastern countryside of 100 years ago, while not true wilderness, was more than wild enough to be sacred. A farmer's cornfield or an overgrown logging road did not disqualify a tract but instead offered character and even some utility. But what has happened in the last 20 years or so is different. Too much land has been stolen for purposes that won't relinquish it to nature for generations to come. I wonder whether any generation of humans will be around to see the inevitable return of true wilderness. Perhaps my spirit will abide here then, having witnessed oceans of time wash over this land but yet seeing it then with the innocent eyes of the child I used to be. These are my woods. As they have changed, so have I. But nothing can change who we are forever.

While they may seem permanent, human marks upon the land will vanish as surely as the scars from a wildfire or windstorm damage.

Reinforced concrete, vinyl siding and PVC pipes may not disappear as fast as the top out of a poplar tree split by lightning, but as measured by nature's clock, all these wounds are but fleeting moments in a progression of states spanning a timeframe we cannot fathom. Does nature's ability to heal itself with vast doses of time make it OK for us to insult its sensibilities as we do? Does it excuse our ignorant and unsustainable ways? No, indeed it does not. But it offers those of us who need it the comfort of knowing that both forgiveness and salvation are coming one day.

Any time spent in the woods is special, but one of the most cathartic, soul-cleansing ways to re-establish perspective between the world we have built, where we spend too much time, and the natural world, where we are but occasional visitors, is to spend an entire day or more in the latter. When I was younger, I had a tradition during the weeklong muzzleloader deer season in West Virginia. Beginning on the first day, I would head into the woods before daylight, usually well before as my destination was often between a half and a full mile from home, and I always arrived before even a hint of daylight. I never used treestands, but instead would climb a good tree, find a quasi-comfortable position and simply stay there all day. Ascending a tree in the black of night, pulling up a gunny sack full of gear and embarking on a 13-hour vigil is not for the faint of heart. It is often cold, usually uncomfortable, but always salubrious in its ability to release one from the madness of life in human society and reconnect him with the natural world.

Sitting in one spot in the woods from before dawn until after dark, seeing nothing but what can be observed from that single vantage point, and watching the slow circuit of time that is a day play out before your eyes have a very real effect on the senses. It slows one down. It's as if your mind and body shift into a different rhythm. The difference is palpable. If, from your vantage point, you can hear the sounds of human society, you begin to notice a grating, dysfunctional aspect to it. Even the sound of traffic is enough to reveal that quality. Revving engines, the regularity with which the tires of hurried drivers squeal around a certain sharp turn, the occasional angry horn blasts that seem to be yelling at everyone and everything within earshot, the way traffic peaks as people scurry off to work and then ebbs through midday before mounting again as they rush home, even the surprisingly short amount of time it takes a vehicle, even a loud one, to enter and leave earshot is testament to how unnaturally fast-paced (and by extension short-sighted) human society is. It's little wonder most people don't comprehend sustainability. Their lives and lifestyles make it nearly impossible for them to do so. It's easy to get sucked into that lifestyle. Almost all of us do, and while we're there, it's very hard to see that other perspective, the one afforded by a visceral connection to the cycles of the natural world.

Embracing Sustainability

Taking that all-day seat in the woods is one way to regain it. Like sleep, the connection can come slowly, or all at once, but you will know when it has arrived. Gone are the urges to look at your watch every 10 minutes for a time check. Burdensome and stressful thoughts leave your mind. Wistful notions and warm, affirming ideas fill the void. There are also extended periods when no discernible concepts of any kind take the mind's stage. Instead, one is aware only of a satisfying sense of well-being arising out of one's surroundings: the purplish white raspberry canes in a nearby thicket, a blown over cherry tree festooned with wild grapes, the small beech still holding vanilla leaves bleached by winter's raw touch, a patch of green grass in the otherwise brown and grey woods—evidence of either a seep or a reliable spot of sunlight through the canopy of summer. These or a hundred other aspects of place conspire to create background noise, an almost audible buzz in an otherwise idle mind, a mind at peace with the wild virtue surrounding it. The movement of the clouds, the track of the sun across the sky, the changing nature of the day as the wet, new feel of morning yields to the strength of midday, which slowly accedes to the muted calm of the approaching eve—these are the primary elements that provide input to a mind properly connected to the natural world. Appointments, deadlines, tasks, responsibilities—the things that fill it at other times—are silly—pointless folly now. That they are all that matter to most people—people who would find irrelevant the perspectives a woodlot affords my soul—provides a glimpse of the enormous impasse that must be overcome if humans are to successfully embrace sustainability.

About 20 years ago, after another muzzleloader season had come to an end, an acquaintance of mine asked me whether I ever felt lonely sitting in the woods all day. My immediate and best answer was that I didn't know because I had never thought about it. The next day, as I drove to work, my eyes glanced into the woods and then back to the yellow line, which I had already begun to cross. Then it hit me. I was returning to a world and a perspective I knew was bankrupt on so many levels. I glanced toward the woods again and wondered what my car sounded like from there. As I hurried along, I knew. What would happen there today that I would not be a part of? I knew that too, and the answer immediately filled me with the most crushing, frantic type of loneliness I had ever felt—a loneliness my friend could never have anticipated in her misaligned query. I've carried that loneliness with me ever since, often reflecting on it and using it as a place marker to always remind me which perspectives and principles matter most in life. You see, loneliness does not come from being separated from the hectic hustle of human civilization. It comes instead from realizing what is lost by participating in it.

Steady State Economics

Economic growth was, far and away, the biggest issue of the 2012 United States election cycle. Every politician, from local all the way to president, talked about it endlessly. So did political pundits and hordes of journalists reporting on the campaigns. All this talk about economic growth was unanimous in declaring such growth would not only be good, but was in fact essential for our well being. Not once did I hear anyone mention steady state economics. It is absolutely astounding that so many intelligent people could be so ignorant to the reality that continued growth is not what our society needs.

Steady state economics simply suggests that the total size of our economy, however we wish to express or calculate it, must stop increasing when or before it reaches the limit of the planet's ability to sustainably provide the inputs needed for that growth. There is not a single wealth-generating institution on this planet that can make money without a commensurate input of the Earth's riches. Attached to all capital is a burden that must be borne on the shoulders of this planet. We ignore this reality today and pretend that our economy operates in a vacuum, separate from nature. Because many of the products produced and sold today are, indeed, artificial, we seem to believe that their existence is not connected to anything natural, but that is not true. Every tangible item that has ever rolled off an assembly line or emerged from a factory is made of materials taken directly or indirectly from the Earth. Shaping them into their final form also takes energy, lots of it, which is predominantly gleaned from fuels, the extraction and use of which also carry a separate toll that our planet has been absorbing. Even service industries and institutions that don't make physical products—say a consulting firm—consume resources to produce capital. To earn a profit, their employees must commute to work, travel to conferences or meetings with clients, produce reports in either paper or electronic form, communicate with one another and maintain or advance their own skills and professional development. Their work is done in office space that also requires a lot of natural resources to create and maintain. Without exception, all economic growth arises from natural resources gleaned from our Earth. There are very real limits to this system. Despite the dreams of capitalism, the generation of wealth cannot be infinite.

I heard several separate news reports in the fall of 2012 discussing the new unemployment data in which an "expert" lamented that the rate of job creation was only a little greater than necessary to keep up with population growth. Neither our overpopulation crisis nor the unsustainable consequences of endless economic growth were mentioned at all, even though both will, with 100 percent certainty, destroy our society if allowed to continue. That fact, which should be obvious, didn't seem to register in the mind of either the experts or the journalists interviewing them.

Politicians and business leaders want the economy to grow even faster than the population. They want this, of course, because it means their profits will increase. But it's not only business leaders who enjoy instant gratification when the economy grows. Most of the rungs of the socio-economic ladder get a shot in the arm when there's a surge in economic activity. Anyone with a 401 K or other investment will benefit. So as with many of the other ways in which our society and lifestyle are unsustainable, economic growth is accompanied by a very sweet reward for doing exactly the wrong thing, and everyone gets to partake of it. The result is that it is probably impossible to convince people to do what needs to be done (stop overall economic growth and actually shrink our GDP).

We have put ourselves in a position that would make ending economic growth incredibly painful. As a global economy dependent on growth, we are not unlike a drug addict who would find withdrawal to be excruciatingly unpleasant. To us, the only thing that feels good is the very thing that is killing us. And like a drug addict, we are in our current predicament because of stupid decisions we made in the past and because we were not able to anticipate consequences and plan responsibly for the future. The industrial revolution offered the euphoric feeling of rapid economic growth. A lot of wealth was generated very quickly, but every dollar of it required the commodification of a share of the Earth's natural resources. Early economists recognized that fact, but somewhere in the hysteria of growth and development, economists have forgotten that the Earth is a variable, in fact the limiting factor, in all economic equations. We will not achieve sustainability without also transitioning to a steady state economy. The two are, in many ways, the same thing.

A True Sustainable Forestry Initiative

You may have heard of the Sustainable Forestry Initiative. SFI is a large organization that serves as a third party monitoring system to determine and then certify that forest-based products are being produced legally, responsibly and, they claim, sustainably. Originally organized to help stop illegally logged trees from making their way into mainstream markets, SFI has expanded in recent years to involve a host of projects and functions related to conservation and forest management. The organization's heart seems to be in the right place, and SFI has no doubt brought a lot of improvements to the areas in which it is involved.

SFI has not, however, brought us to a point where our forestry practices are sustainable. Like hunters, loggers often suffer from the unfair reputation that what they do is fundamentally wrong. The truth is that harvesting both game animals and trees can be done sustainably. However, in the case of the latter, even the most conscientious and well-intentioned loggers today are not doing so.

The forest products industry is a significant fixture in the Southern, Northwestern and Northeastern United States, and the people who make their living from it believe wholeheartedly in what they do. Most of them care about the woods and would not want their practices to harm the forests in which they live and work. In some cases, three or four generations of the same family have made their livings cutting trees in and around the places they live. They want to believe that what they do is sustainable, and from what they can see, it appears as if it is. Organizations such as SFI validate their hopes, but the truth is, it is not sustainable to remove most of the mature timber mass from a tract of land on a regular basis anymore than it is sustainable to cut hay from the same field year after year without adding fertilizer of some kind.

Whether it's orchard grass in a hayfield or an oak tree in a forest, all plants grow in similar ways. Much of the mass they acquire as they grow is water taken up by their roots and carbon taken out of the air as carbon dioxide by their leaves. But water and carbon are not the only inputs that go into making a blade of grass or a sawlog. A small fraction of the mass of either comes from minerals—phosphorous, nitrogen, potassium, magnesium and others—that are found in the soil. In the natural world, trees and grass die and decompose, returning all the nutrients they took up, plus a little more. This little bit of extra nutrients adds imperceptibly to the soil every year. Like the pennies of interest earned by a modern day savings account, the meager annual addition of soil nutrients adds up over the centuries.

When a farmer begins to cut hay from a fertile field, he is dipping into the interest accrued over thousands of years of compounding. For a few years, the grass will spring up strong and tall, and each year, the farmer will cut it, convinced that he can harvest it this way indefinitely. But somewhere between year five and ten, he will notice a steady decline in production. The minerals in the soil are being depleted because they are being removed faster than they can be replenished. It is unsustainable.

An identical process unfolds when timber is harvested. The decline will not be noticeable in 10 years as it would be in a hayfield. Tress are harvested in cycles of 20 to 80 years, so declines in soil quality and productivity may not occur for several human generations, but rest assured, if harvesting would continue as it currently is in commercially managed forests for 100,000 years, what are today rich woodlands would have long since been reduced to impoverished scrubland, incapable of growing anything but brush. Repeatedly taking wood from the land without giving anything back is unsustainable. Therefore, even wood produced under the SFI system is not truly sustainable.

The solution is simply to put back at least as much as is taken. Most forestry professionals consider fertilizing forests to be impractical, but it would be interesting to see what they might think of the idea if they could be transported thousands of years into the future and see what will become of regularly harvested forests without some method of replacing nutrients. A sustainable system must envision nutrient exchange as a chemistry equation that must remain in balance. Everything taken out must be put back. The most honest, natural way to achieve this equilibrium is to return wood to the forests from whence it came. Most timber harvested in America goes into paper products, construction materials or furniture. When these items reach the end of their useful life, they should be chipped or shredded and returned to the forest floor, where they can decompose and return their nutrients to the ground.

Recycling these materials is just as good as returning them to the ground, because recycling prevents an equal amount of timber from being harvested somewhere else. Delaying the removal of nutrients does as much good as putting nutrients back, but unfortunately, very few of these wood products are recycled when their useful life is over. Most are sent to a landfill, which has the effect of stealing nutrients from the forest soil and sequestering them in a tomb.

If we're capable of getting timber out of a forest, then we're capable of putting it back after we're finished using it. Like most of our other problems with sustainability, willpower is all we're lacking. A zero-landfill society would need to find something else to do with a lot of wood debris anyhow, so putting it back where it came from would be a perfect solution. It's a simple matter to keep track of the volume of wood removed from a certain area and then ensure that an equal volume of chipped or shredded wood waste is returned to the area. Nobody does this kind of thing now, and most would scoff at it as a downright weird idea. That reaction is evidence of how far removed our current attitudes are from a worldview that embraces sustainability. It would cost more to return forest products to the place of their origin than it does to simply throw them away. It would also be less convenient. But sustainability does not bow to the altar of profit or convenience the way our contemporary society does. Instead, sustainability values processes and practices that will pass the test of time—a criterion few people consider today.

The answer is not chemical fertilizers, which themselves are unsustainable. Even manure or other natural fertilizer is not as good a choice as returning wood mass to the forests because any other source of nutrients must have come from somewhere else. Using them to enrich forests means that land in another place is being depleted to accomplish that goal. Any transaction we undertake involving nutrients must balance like a company's petty cash account. Resources taken from one place must be replaced with something of equal value.

If we intend to someday return the wood we harvest to the forests that provided it, it will be important that we stop painting, sealing, impregnating and treating it with chemicals we would not also want in the soil. There are lots of reasons that every substance we introduce into the Earth should be as benign as the natural elements and compounds we used to concoct it. Respecting the notion that our Earth is not a receptacle for toxic waste will pay many dividends, including being able to return wood mass to the forests from which we borrowed it.

To be deserving of the title "sustainable forestry," our timbering activities would need to be powered exclusively by renewable energy. That means trucks, heavy equipment, even saws would need to be powered by renewables. Right now, that means batteries charged by solar or wind electricity. Equipment would need hydraulic fluid and gear oil not derived from fossil fuels. Likewise, chain saws would need to use something other than petroleum-based bar oil for chain lubrication.

Sawmills and kilns would also need to be zero-carbon, zero landfill affairs, powered by renewable energy. The more local we could keep our wood, the better. Timber grown and used in the same approximate area would be ideal because fewer resources would be needed for transportation.

The idea of doing absolutely everything necessary to ensure our use of wood does not deplete the nutrients forests need, even if we continue to cut for thousands of generations, is not a bizarre idea. We already have a name for it and an organization that claims to exist for that purpose. With the right approach to harvesting wood, we could have a true Sustainable Forestry Initiative.

Have You Ever Wondered?

Have you ever wondered what it would be like to live in a primitive time, before the enlightened understanding we have today? If so, you may have imagined doctors wanting to drain all the blood out of your body if you became sick, thinking that it would cure you. You may have imagined a time when people thought the Earth was the center of the solar system or was flat and would persecute you if you disagreed with them. Or how about living in a time and place where human sacrifices were made to appease the gods? If you think the ignorance of such conditions would drive you out of your mind, you better hold on to your sanity as tightly as you can because our current situation is only slightly better. Plenty of people still oppose sound science because they believe at some level that it conflicts with something they hold dear.

Just as in earlier times when primitive societies would not hear of heliocentrism or would have thought medicine was black magic, there are many today who are downright combative toward concepts such as evolution, climate change and, yes, sustainability. Just try suggesting to some that the human fertility rate needs to be between 1 and 2. Upon learning what you mean, they will want to fight you, not because they have evidence that you are wrong, but just because they hate your ideas, and by extension, you.

Plenty of people openly support the idea of landfills. Just the other day, someone commented to me that "we still have plenty of room for landfills." I suppose he meant we should continue using them until there was no place on Earth that wasn't filled with garbage and only at that point, consider an alternative. The individual who made that comment is someone most people would regard as educated and intelligent. He holds a professional position and is well above average in socio-economic status. But on issues of sustainability, he is a Neanderthal. Unfortunately, his thinking is typical of most Americans.

As a society, we blithely condone a plastic, throwaway lifestyle powered by non-renewable fossil fuels. We watch with all the understanding of a cow pondering a wildflower as biodiversity retreats in the wake of our inefficient, wasteful lifestyles. By living like there's no tomorrow, we have put ourselves on a collision course with extinction, and yet we consider ourselves the most intelligent, most accomplished life form in our planet's history. Have you ever wondered how future civilizations will view ours? I'm thinking they won't be nearly as impressed with our accomplishments as we seem to be.

Evenflow or Evanesce

Since the agricultural and industrial revolutions, humans have been able to increase their reproductive rates far beyond what they would have achieved in prehistoric times, and it has led to rampant overpopulation. If we are to survive as a species, we have got to get a handle on our population. For eons, pre-industrial humans seemed to live sustainably. Will we ever again find stasis, or are we incapable of voluntarily obeying the laws of population dynamics? Does our lust for technology make it impossible for us to play by the same rules as all other living things? All the plant and animal species I know of are held in check by predation or limits to needed resources, not some great powers of self-control. Given the opportunity, most species would surely overpopulate at least temporarily. We have given ourselves that chance; predation and disease have been greatly curtailed, and with technology, we have artificially, if temporarily, multiplied the resources that support us. We have allowed ourselves admission to paradise—an existence free of the tribulations that dog the rest of life on Earth. But with the ability to lift from ourselves the restraints that hold the populations of other living things in check must come the duty of making sure our Eden can last.

If humanity is going to have a serious conversation about population, we have to decide it's not a taboo subject. Few Americans have ever thought about human overpopulation. If someone brings it to their attention, they usually react by deciding the person is deranged or wants to start trucking people off to the gas chamber. For many, no matter how carefully the topic is framed, overpopulation will remain a subject of conversation to be avoided at all costs. Such a reality doesn't bode well for the prospects of meaningful progress on the issue.

Biological evolution will not save us. If certain populations of humans come to manage their numbers successfully and avoid the destruction that will befall their reckless brethren, it will be a social, not biological, characteristic that accounts for the difference. So how do we decide to agree that overpopulation is an issue that needs our attention? Coercive legislation is not the answer, and is doomed to fail. Somehow, the people of the world (or at least those autonomous units that want to survive) will need to decide for themselves that human population needs to be managed as carefully as every other aspect of society. The fire marshal can decide with precise certainty the maximum occupancy of a restaurant or conference hall. No one objects to such determinations because everyone agrees that it's in our best interest to avoid the dangers of overcrowding in public spaces. Well, the Earth is a public space, but trying to set a number for the maximum occupancy of the Earth would result in howls of objection. Only when that type of reaction ends will there be hope for managing our numbers. So how might we get there? Will the mounting pain of overpopulation finally cause us to yield like someone pulling back his hand from a flame, or will our impossibly unwieldy society simply collapse, preventing us from continuing to add more floors to our house of cards? The choice is ours; we can evenflow, or we can evanesce.

A Bug's Life

The emerald ash borer is an invasive insect getting a lot of attention for the damage it is inflicting on white ash trees in the Eastern United States. Some predict ash trees will go the way of the chestnut—virtually eliminated by the side effects of another life form's activities.

Although most people would consider themselves and humans in general to be infinitely more sophisticated, intelligent and wise than a beetle, the similarities between our approach to existing and that of the ash borer are undeniable. Both we and they are killing the resource that makes our own life possible. The ash borer is killing ash trees, and we are killing the Earth. Emerald ash borers seem incapable of utilizing any tree but white ash. They bore holes into the limbs and trunk of the tree, which eventually dies when sufficiently perforated. What will they do if their activities drive ash trees to near extinction? The answer is simple: Their numbers will crash as well. If an emerald ash borer could think and speak, it might likely say, "I've been drilling holes my entire life and there are still ash trees. Besides, all trees die eventually, and new trees always grow in their place. The forest has been here forever. It's too big for me to harm in any significant way." And so emerald ash borers and humans are behaving in remarkably similar ways, foolishly depleting the very things they must have to survive. An even more ironic element of the story is the fact that ash borers wouldn't be devastating ash trees in North America if humans hadn't stupidly introduced them to that continent from their home in Asia.

The white ash has evolved along with the other species of northern hardwoods over hundreds of thousands of years. Emerald ash borers arrived on the scene in North America less than 20 years ago. Blissfully unaware of concepts such as time and sustainability, the speaking ash borer might continue, "My parents and grandparents also drilled holes in ash trees, and the world didn't come to an end." And like humans, the ash borer might try to rationalize behavior that is threatening the future for all as necessary for the well-being of its own offspring. "I have larvae who are depending on me to provide a place for them to live and grow. That's more important than some trees." And so in an attempt to ensure success for itself and its progeny, the ash borer is actually ensuring the eventual failure of its own species. The only way for the ash borer to avoid this fate is to change its lifestyle and utilize ash trees in a way that does not kill them or cause their numbers to decrease—in other words, achieve sustainability.

The type of struggle for equilibrium going on now between the white ash tree and the emerald ash borer is not new or unusual. Evolution has served as the judge at many such trials over the eons. The case of the emerald ash borer versus the ash tree will be decided soon. If the ash borer wants to be part of the forest ecosystem, it will need to play a sustainable role. Evolution will see to it. But meanwhile, there is another case on the docket with very similar circumstances. It also involves a very new life form that is using up resources it needs much more quickly than they can be replenished. This species, which has named itself Homo sapiens, claims that it must live this way in order to have a satisfactory existence. Most members of the species deny there is any problem with their lifestyle. Like the speaking ash borer, individuals of this species become defensive if someone points out the unsustainable nature of their lifestyle. They resent the suggestion that they can't live however they want. But they cannot. Like it or not, nature will not tolerate unsustainability, be it from humans or ash borers. For both these species, time will tell if they stay or if they go. Ash borers are completely at the mercy of the laws of population ecology. Humans allegedly have free will to plan their destiny. Does anyone want to take bets on the outcome?

Sustainability and the Passenger Pigeon

With the 100th anniversary of the extinction of the passenger pigeon upon us (Sept. 1, 2014), it's depressing to see how few people even know what a passenger pigeon was or what happened to them. Even after being told, most people don't seem to be too impressed as the many lessons about overconsumption, waste and sustainability wash over them. Instead, most stare blankly back and seem to be wondering why they needed to know about this. The underwhelmed response of the average person to the story of the passenger pigeon does not change, however, the fact that it is full of valuable stuff to ponder relative to sustainability.

The first area that's fascinating to think about is how the passenger pigeon evolved as it did and how it achieved sustainability and ecological balance as a species. To say that the passenger pigeon's population was huge is no understatement. Massive flocks, estimated by reliable observers to number in the billions, would block out the sun for days as they passed overhead. No other species of bird even came close to matching their numbers. Why did the passenger pigeon evolve to attain such numbers? All species of living things seem to try to exist in as great a quantity as the resources that support them will allow. Given perfect conditions, any species will increase its population size—indefinitely if the right conditions could be provided. But the real world is not a set of perfect conditions. Food is limited, and there's competition for it. Predation is a constant downward force, especially for an animal like a passenger pigeon. Lots of predators would have found them attractive. Disease and weather also place limits on population and are among the reasons mortality rates are usually higher than 50 percent in the first year for birds. So what niche did the passenger pigeon find that allowed it to benefit from vast resources while seemingly experiencing little resistance in the form of either predation or competition? It ate the same foods as many other forest animals and would have been equally desirable as prey for whatever predator, avian or mammalian, might be interested in a medium sized bird for a meal. So how did its population swell to such a great size while the populations of so many other animals found it impossible to do likewise?

Passenger pigeons migrated, but that is hardly unique. They reproduced in vast nesting colonies that would overwhelm predators in any given area, but that strategy is common in nature as well, and it doesn't explain how they got to be that way in the first place. The colonies were vast because of the great number of birds in them, but how did the birds manage to amass such great populations to begin with? Unless you believe in a literal interpretation of creation, billions of passenger pigeons were not simply deposited into the woodlands of North America overnight. Passenger pigeons evolved right alongside most every other animal they shared an ecosystem with, except the passenger pigeon seemed to be far more successful than any other in terms of achieving a huge but sustainable population. How did they do it? The descriptions of passenger pigeon flocks from the 16th century sound incredible. The birds would roost in such numbers as to break down most of the trees in the forest for miles. The result was said to look like damage from a tornado or hurricane. In a matter of days, their excrement would accumulate in thick layers and kill all the understory in a forest. Their vast numbers and the accompanying destruction they brought were plague-like in proportion. The accounts of people who witnessed the nesting and roosting habits of the passenger pigeon, which experts today agree were accurate and reliable, sound very much like descriptions of some invasive species that had recently overrun an area in which it had previously never existed. Usually, such population outbursts from an invasive species are short lived—resources are depleted, causing population levels to shrink, and native plants and animals adapt, restoring a more balanced albeit altered state to the ecosystem. But there is no evidence that the passenger pigeon was an interloper, new to the North American scene when Europeans or even Native Americans first came to this continent. The scientific community agrees that passenger pigeons were a part of the native fauna and had existed here for hundreds of thousands of years. That means the tremendous population of the passenger pigeon was sustainable.

The biological largesse that was the passenger pigeon was an example of nature flexing its muscles and becoming as large as an intricate system of checks and balances would allow. But what were the checks and balances governing passenger pigeon populations? We'll never know for sure because the people of that era were more interested in annihilating them than studying them, but to grow and support that much pigeon mass required equally bountiful food supplies. Passenger pigeons ate primarily red oak acorns and beech nuts. The mast of the American chestnut, now pretty much gone from North American forests itself, was extremely plentiful at the time of the passenger pigeon. Experts believe chestnut was the most common tree in the forest across large areas of eastern North America. Perhaps the great proliferation of chestnuts was due, in part, to the pigeon's help in suppressing oak and beech, which would have competed with the chestnut for space in the forest. I have read reliable accounts that claim pigeons ate chestnuts, which is surprising given the size of a chestnut relative to a passenger pigeon's head. Regardless of which nuts pigeons ate most, the real mystery is how passenger pigeons were able to capitalize such vast quantities of valuable mast despite or without competition from other wildlife. No one studied interspecific competition between passenger pigeons and other animals. One thing is for sure, deer, elk, bear, wild turkeys and even blue jays coexisted with passenger pigeons and would have eaten oak and beech nuts as well. How did the passenger pigeon evolve to best them all and become the dominant consumer of that resource? Perhaps that will always remain a mystery, reminding us there's much we don't know about the clockwork of life on Earth.

Equally thought-provoking, to me, is the reproductive strategy of the passenger pigeon. They laid only one egg, which is very uncommon for birds. Most doves and pigeons lay two eggs. The band-tailed pigeon and red-billed pigeon usually lay one egg but are known to lay two. Only the California condor (itself a narrow escapee of extinction), the black swift, northern fulmar, Manx shearwater, four species of storm-petrels, magnificent frigatebird, and the northern gannet will never lay more than one egg per nest. That's 10 birds out of hundreds of species in North America. According to most ornithology textbooks, clutch size (the number of eggs in a nest) is an evolutionarily determined number set to maximize the reproductive success of the female over her lifetime. Laying only one egg is rare simply because most birds can do better than that, and so they do. For most birds, resources are ample but mortality rates are high so they must lay several eggs (and thanks to the ample resources, are able to do so pretty easily). Some bird species exist in a very narrow niche, and their populations cannot grow beyond those limits. Others do find it very hard to secure the resources to successfully raise large numbers of offspring. For these species, clutch size must be smaller. Given the mortality rates among most birds, one egg would not be enough for most species to even maintain their population levels, but it worked for the passenger pigeon. Even if 100 percent of the young survived to adulthood, which never happens, every living pair of passenger pigeons would have had to successfully nest and fledge a squab two years in a row just to keep their population size stable. Given the inevitability of some reproductive failure, the average passenger pigeon must have successfully nested more than two times to maintain a population equilibrium. This must have been their Achilles' heel. They must have needed very high rates of nesting success to maintain their numbers. When humans began to significantly disrupt their nesting success, attrition quickly did the pigeons in. It seems to me that passenger pigeons evolved the strict one-egg strategy because reproducing at any greater rate would have been unsustainable. Presumably, had passenger pigeons laid two eggs like other doves and pigeons, their population would have quickly grown too large for the resource base that supported it. That they needed such a restrictive reproductive system (by bird standards) to keep from exceeding the carrying capacity of the land is more evidence of how successful the passenger pigeon must have been in overcoming challenges that other animals found significantly more difficult. Imagine, a bird that only lays one egg being able to maintain a population more numerous than the populations of all other bird species put together. Most bird species would quickly go extinct if limited to a clutch size of one, but for the passenger pigeon, it was the right formula for sustainability. There's a great lesson there for humans, if anyone cares to listen.

Did the passenger pigeon's one-egg strategy come before their evolution as a species or did it happen sometime later, as their populations began to increase? It seems unlikely to have been a later adaptation, because how would individually lower reproductive rates be adaptive? Of course, using that logic, how would a one-egg strategy ever have developed in any species? Other doves and pigeons lay one or two eggs, but never more. It seems passenger pigeons would have had the one-egg strategy from their beginning, something inherited from a common ancestor, but how did a bird with such a low reproductive rate and seemingly equal challenges of finding food and avoiding predators come to be able to amass such huge numbers when other species of doves or pigeons didn't or couldn't? It's such a complicated question. Evolution is a complex mystery, and when its results stymie our imagination, perhaps the best conclusion for us to draw is the need for us to remain humble—to not challenge, meddle with or disrespect the magnificence of life on Earth. We believe ourselves to be smart, but clearly, the clockwork of life is beyond our cognition.

Surely, passenger pigeon population numbers would increase and decrease over time as they remained locked in an intricate dance with the resources that supported them. I wonder if their numbers were cyclical as some species are, increasing until they began to suppress their food source, then declining until the resource rebounded? Given the way they would travel around almost nomadically, going wherever food was plentiful, it seems less likely they would have undergone cycles in that way. But I bet they did vary over eons. Ice ages, I'm sure, cut into their numbers as huge area that had been forest would be locked under glacial ice. But then when the glaciers retreated, I'm sure their numbers would increase as the forests returned. Passenger pigeons were probably responsible for helping forests march northward again after ice ages, spreading seeds much faster than they could otherwise disburse.

Some of the most fascinating mysteries related to passenger pigeons and sustainability have to do with their ecological role and their relationships with other species that shared the same ecosystem. Ruffed grouse, American woodcock and many other bird species require young, early successional forest habitat. When forests mature, these birds decline greatly or vanish altogether. Fire, wind storms and other natural disturbances do not seem to have been particularly effective in keeping Eastern hardwood forests young.

Mature forests seem to prevail wherever they are allowed to do so, and most stories of forests in colonial times suggest large, unbroken tracks of mature, old-growth timber. But yet Native Americans apparently knew ruffed grouse well and early accounts of hunting by settlers report them to have been numerous although not particularly wary. It is well documented that Native Americans cleared land, often by burning, for the express purpose of improved hunting, but I wonder if passenger pigeons also contributed to the vitality of young forests though their roosting and nesting habits. Passenger pigeon roosting and nesting areas were very large, usually miles in length and breadth, and reports indicate that their activity would significantly disturb much of these large areas, both by physically breaking down trees and branches and by the killing of vegetation from thick deposits of acidic manure. The result may have been even more thorough destruction than from either wildfire or windstorm, and would undoubtedly have resulted in good early successional habitat for ruffed grouse and similar animals when the woods regrew. If every year, one or more nesting colonies created several square miles of early successional habitat in this way, many species that depend on young forests would have owed a great deal of their success to the passenger pigeon. Without passenger pigeons to create these disturbances in the forest, early successional species would begin to decline. One of the ecological voids left by the extinction of the passenger pigeon may have been a decline in habitat for early successional species. At first, heavy logging in the 19th and early 20th century probably delayed this impact, but now that clearcutting is not widely practiced and fire is suppressed, there is little to reset the forest clock and create young woods. This lack of early successional habitat is becoming a very noticeable problem in many parts of the Eastern United States. If the passenger pigeon were still around, that might not be the case.

    Without a doubt, anything as big as the passenger pigeon population must have made a huge ecological "splash in the pond," both in life and in extinction, but the effects of their extinction may have been covered up or clouded by other ecological changes (all human induced such as deforestation and market hunting) taking place at the same time. It seems that losing something as large as the passenger pigeon would leave a tremendous ecological vacuum that other species would rush in to fill. Should deer, turkey, squirrel, bear or other species have increased as a result of the resources no longer being utilized by the pigeons? It sounds plausible, but perhaps that's not how it works in real life. Perhaps the loss of the passenger pigeon was greeted with nothing more than the emptiness it created, a lonely gray consequence to remind us of the cost of our actions. Perhaps it is we humans, with our urban sprawl, who usurped much of the resource base vacated by the loss of the passenger pigeon. Experts agree that the Eastern

United States could never again support something as biologically massive as the migrating flocks of billions of passenger pigeons, primarily because the vast Eastern forests are now but a patchwork of their former glory. The true ecological impact of the passenger pigeon's extinction will probably remain a mystery. It was not studied in detail as it occurred, and now that chance, like the pigeon itself, is gone forever.

So many questions related to sustainability and the passenger pigeon remain. Why did they exist in such huge numbers? They must have had some sort of advantage or superiority over other life forms. Nature does not bestow that degree of success randomly or by accident. It must be earned and deserved. And why then, if passenger pigeons were especially well suited to overcome challenges placed before them, did they go extinct when, by all accounts, many thousands remained by the time heavy hunting pressure subsided in the late 1800s? Lots of species have recovered from the brink of extinction with far fewer individuals remaining in the wild. Perhaps somehow, the same mysterious element that allowed them to exist in such great numbers also prevented them from doing so on a smaller scale. Their unique adaptation for success, whatever it was, also made them inflexible in ways that are hard to comprehend. Still though, it must be remembered that they would never have been challenged in such an unfair way if not for our blasphemous assault.

Why, if so successful in North America, did they not populate the forests of South America as well? It would seem an easy, almost likely, thing for them to do—follow the forests of Central America until they open into the vast Brazilian jungle and beyond. Surely they could have adapted to whatever mast is produced there. They had eons of time to do so. It's fascinating to contemplate such mysteries, but the answers will probably never be ours. Whatever authority orchestrates the grandeur of life on Earth was satisfied with the impressive stature the passenger pigeon achieved in North America. The forests of the southern hemisphere were reserved for the glorious carnival of life that filled those places with unique local color. If we find ourselves confused by reality, if we fail to comprehend what and why certain things are or were, the deficit lies in our perception and nowhere else.

How did passenger pigeons change over their evolutionary history? Did they evolve slowly or rapidly or somewhere in between? What did their early ancestors look like? Were they smaller or larger? Which adaptations became more prominent as they approached the form we knew—their final iteration? The fossil record contains evidence of passenger pigeons as far back as 100,000 years ago, but how far back did they really go? Would passenger pigeons of 500,000 years ago, if they existed as a species then, be more or less similar to 18th century pigeons than our ancestors from 500,000 years ago were to 18th century humans?

Embracing Sustainability

Of course, any discussion of sustainability and the passenger pigeon must eventually come to focus on the actions of humans that led to their extinction. How ironic it is that an animal so numerous and so visible as the passenger pigeon could become and would be allowed to become a victim of human annihilation. One thing we now know is that extinction is not impossible. If we can do it to the passenger pigeon, we can do it to anything. We humans could also find ourselves in an un-survivable situation more easily that we might imagine or believe. How easily we forget. One of the biggest lessons from the passenger pigeon debacle is that in less than 100 years, almost all trace of the episode has faded from the collective consciousness. What percentage of Americans think about the story and the lessons of the passenger pigeon on a regular basis? I would say it's incredibly low and getting smaller all the time. There has been very little cultural learning. Yes, there are laws and a conservation movement that are partly or wholly the result of the passenger pigeon experience, but individually, too few people have a personal awareness of lessons learned from that era. The American Revolution in the late 1700s and our Civil War in the mid 1800s are two events that took place at the same time the passenger pigeon was being exploited and driven to extinction. Knowledge about the American Revolutionary War and the Civil War are common. Plenty of Americans will explain that their perceptions of such topics as freedom, liberty and equality are rooted in what they know about those wars. The history classes taught in every high school in the nation ensure that it is so. But lessons learned about conservation and sustainability from the same period have not carried forward as strongly. One of the most powerful life forces on the planet was snuffed out only 100 years ago, but even that immense blow did little to awaken our collective awareness. What will it take? Are we even capable of learning about sustainability, or will our ways prove as unalterably fatal to us as they did to the passenger pigeon?

The final lesson to embrace from the passenger pigeon debacle is that all unnatural extinctions are shameful and inexcusable. The passenger pigeon was larger than life. Its annihilation could not go unnoticed, at least at the time. But many, many more species, most of them unknown, are silently going the way of the passenger pigeon, fading into oblivion in the wake of human civilization. Few people know how many species are being lost or the extent of the sixth mass extinction our planet is now undergoing. A small frog in the Amazon no one has ever seen may not seem as important as the passenger pigeon (and indeed may fill a less prominent ecological role), but who are we to judge the worth of a species? What are we humans worth, as a species, to the rest of life on Earth? The many "smaller" extinctions for which we are responsible are adding up, and we will carry their weight, along with that of the passenger pigeon, on our shoulders forever.

Time to be Smart

It's frustrating to see what's wrong with a deeply flawed system but to be powerless to correct it. We are not truly free if we are conscribed to watch our society and our species self-destruct out of laziness and ignorance. We are not truly free if we are forced to participate in such a pathetic existence. Even worse is the notion that one's current family and future progeny are also condemned to that fate. What should those who recognize the unsustainability of our current society do? How should they channel their urge to right things when society is simply not ready or willing to change yet? In addition to continuing to speak the truth, the only good choice seems to be finding a way to create a legacy of sustainability for one's own family. Instead of feeling regret or remorse, the smart choice is to take the kind of action now that will put your own family on a path to sustainability. Maybe all that's needed is for someone (or several someones) to begin the job. Then, once people notice the work that's being done, more and more will roll up their sleeves and join in. Lots of struggles begin as seemingly impossible challenges, grassroots initiatives that get increasingly easier as they become mainstream. Figuring a way to carve a sustainable existence out of an unsustainable society is both logistically and operationally difficult, but it's time to be smart and figure it out.

Coal is Murder

If you want to feel sad, angry and incredulous all at the same time, stand in a forest that is scheduled to be strip mined in the near future. First, a wave of sadness will wash over you when you realize what will be lost. Untold species of animals—birds, mammals, amphibians, reptiles and insects—will either be displaced or killed when the heavy machines begin their sadistic work. And as for the plants, they will all perish. A perfect garden of broadleaf plants, shrubs and trees will be torn asunder, pushed into mounds like trash, and burned. Irreplaceable topsoil, rich with just the right mix of minerals and microbes, will be ripped away like the skin from a corpse. The coal company will claim to save the topsoil if the terrain permits—piling it up for later replacement. But there's not a reclaimed strip mine on Earth where this exquisite topsoil has been put back right. The difference is instantly obvious, as what is returned usually contains more clay and rock fragments than anything else. "Spoil" is what this material is called. It's an apt name for the entire process. The perverted biology left in the wake of a strip mine—just invasive plants and a miniscule fraction of the animal life present previously, is sickening to anyone who understands what's been lost and knows its true value.

Next, anger creeps in around the sadness when you realize how needless and preventable the impending tragedy really is. It doesn't have to be this way, if only reason and common sense would prevail. But they won't, and when that realization sinks in, a hopeless sense of dismay crashes down squarely on top of you. What kind of crazy world is this anyway? Like an episode of "The Twilight Zone," you stand trapped in a bizarre and tortuous reality that doesn't seem like reality at all. How can an enlightened society be so blind as to condone a practice as patently wrong on every level as strip mining?

The source of incredulity and dismay some of us feel is that so many others see the before and after of a strip mine as equivalent or virtually so. They see the murder of an ecosystem as a fair trade for a temporary supply of energy. And so not only do those who understand have to witness an atrocity, but they must do so alone, abandoned by a society that doesn't care and surrounded only by people who display either ambivalence or even support for the terrible wrong being committed. It's a wrong borne of greed and abetted by ignorance. It's also a wrong that cannot and will not last. It is unsustainable. But how bad will things need to get before a majority receive the wake-up call? How much land will be murdered? How many sacred places will be destroyed before a corner is turned? The dark ages lasted 1,000 years. We have enough coal left for less than half that amount of time, so surely our suffering won't be measured in millennia. Perhaps we can prevail in only another generation or two. It will take much change, but it can be done. Our renaissance is coming. What, unfortunately, can never be done is to right the wrongs already committed. Murder is forever, and the millions of acres of pristine Earth that have been murdered in the name of coal are now lost to us for geologic time. The Earth is a smaller place—literally and figuratively—because of the crimes of the past. It will be even smaller yet when our children someday tally the crimes we commit today.

Ground to Dust

"The question is, does the educated citizen know he is only a cog in an ecological mechanism? That if he will work with that mechanism, his mental wealth and his material wealth can expand indefinitely? But if he refuses to work with it, it will ultimately grind him to dust?"—Aldo Leopold.

Achieving sustainability will require finding ways to survive that don't involve "resource friction"—an escalating contest of wills between us and the planet on which we live. Living that way is as impossible as bootstrapping. Obtaining and using the resources we need to survive should not put us at odds with the planet. The concept of manifest destiny prevalent during frontier times pitted us against the natural world and characterized the latter as an obstacle to be overcome and a threat to be conquered. Nothing could be further from reality. The natural world is all we have. It gives us life and lets us keep it. Availing ourselves of that gift should not involve assaulting the benefactor. The rate at which we enjoy the Earth's gifts must also be cued to coincide with the periodicity of their renewal. Like running a marathon, we must find a pace for life that is not self-destructive.

Instead, we are like foolish young heirs who have just inherited great wealth. Rather than conserving it and carefully planning how to best handle it, we are squandering it on every frivolous use that comes to mind. What will we do when it's gone? The lifestyle to which we have become accustomed will soon come to an abrupt end, leaving us shocked and wishing for a way to regain what we've lost.

Our future can proceed in two possible ways. One is orderly and continues our tradition of using technology to do things we otherwise could not. But instead of applying our technological leverage toward laziness, greed and self-gratification, we will use it to achieve sustainability first and comfort second. Everything we do in this future will be measured against the metric of sustainability. Sustainability will be seen as the essential first attribute of any policy or practice, and we won't rest until that criteria has been applied and met in all we do.

If we don't seriously pursue sustainability, we will find ourselves in the other possible version of the future. Without sustainable pathways for living, much of what we have built modern society upon will collapse as will the human population. Those surviving will find the human condition based in chaos, anarchy and subsistence. Human survival will depend largely on luck and in many ways will resemble life before the rise of classical civilization, when humans moving out of Africa were populating Europe and Asia. The only difference will be that those humans were moving into areas teeming with life and fertility, fully functional ecosystems and seemingly inexhaustible resources. The next time around, humans will find only the wastelands left by the preceding populations. Instead of rich topsoil like that found 5,000 years ago by the humans who developed agriculture in the Fertile Crescent, they will find depleted fields useless without the magic of industrial fertilizer and GMO seed it now takes to produce crops on this exhausted land. Instead of clean water, they will find the soiled leachate of our coal mines, landfills and industrial/chemical factories. Instead of a bounty of wild game, fish and plants, they will feel a hunger born of diminished ecosystems, lost biodiversity and invasive species. In short, the next time humans find themselves as nomads, they will have a much harder time of it than our ancestors did. The humans most likely to succeed (survive) will be those living closest to that way now. There are said to be tribes in the Amazon who have scarcely or never glimpsed human outsiders. They live completely unaware of what humans have done elsewhere on Earth, and may scarcely miss a beat when civilization collapses. The rest of us though, those dependent on an unsustainable civilization for all our survival needs, will be the first ones ground to dust.

Earth and Space

Gazing up at the stars on a clear night, it is hard not to be amazed at the vast size of the universe. Distances that must be measured in light years challenge the limits of human comprehension. That we have yet to find extraterrestrial life on another planet like our own is a testament to the great size of the cosmos. Our Milky Way galaxy alone is so huge, it boggles the mind. There must be life out there, lots of it.

Anyone who has ever flown over the Canadian wilderness in a bush plane can attest to the great number of lakes and ponds visible from the air. Some are big, and some are small. Some are deep and others shallow. Their shapes and shorelines vary. An experienced eye can pick out the ones likely to offer good fishing and also spot the ones that probably would not. Not all of the water seen from the air will be teeming with perch, trout or grayling, but a lot of it will, and if you keep looking, you're bound to spot some with better fishing than you've ever experienced. Scanning the stars for life is, I imagine, much the same. Not every spot will hold it. Much of space is too hot or too cold for any life we can imagine, but there are so many places in between that the odds of finding extraterrestrial life are, I suspect, even greater than the odds of finding fish in Canada!

Staring up at the stars at night, knowing with certainty that the cosmos is an endless swirling mass full of life, offers some degree of comfort to someone disgusted with the offenses being committed against the life of this planet. Every one of the innumerable outposts of life in the cosmos is out of our reach—too far for us to know about, let alone impact. I am glad for the unknown life that surely exists in the "secret" places of the cosmos. I wish this life well and hope that it is flourishing. It, too, is just as much a part of nature as the life on Earth. I am glad that the vast distances of the cosmos have insulated that life from human destruction. The natural resources of those places are safe from us, as we are likely only to develop the ability to reach them if we first learn to live sustainably ourselves, here on Earth. I hope also that life in the cosmos is free from any other dark forces that would disrupt its natural order or diminish its vibrance.

Those who discount extraterrestrial life insist that the Earth is unique in all of creation. I hope that, in one respect, they are right. I hope Earth is the only place where one life form has evolved in such a way as to seriously threaten the existence of not only itself, but much of the other local life as well. Unfortunately, it's probably not. It seems statistically improbable that any aspect of life on Earth is unique or even rare. Perhaps unsustainable civilizations are just a normal part of the evolutionary process once life forms anywhere achieve higher intelligence and the ability to develop technology. Not all random mutations are beneficial. Many are selected against when they reduce fitness. Perhaps modern humans and all that makes us unique will go down in evolutionary history as a failure. Perhaps the differences that spontaneously set us apart from our ancestors will soon lead to our destruction. It is true that the attributes of a society or civilization, such as being sustainable or unsustainable, are not physical adaptations of individual members of a species. As such, they do not equate directly into biological evolution as we commonly think of it. But theories of social evolution suggest the same rules apply—new approaches are tried, with successful strategies retained and unsuccessful ones struck down.

Just as biological evolution proceeds slowly over generations, distinguishing between successful and unsuccessful social adaptations can take time. Strategies that appear to be highly successful at first can ultimately prove to be disastrous failures. Our currently unsustainable human condition could be one such foray into the crucible of evolution. Those uniquely human attributes that set us apart from and allowed us to outcompete other early hominids (superior mastery of technology and an accompanying increase in reproductive success) may be the same attributes that prove to be our undoing. Perhaps we will need to try again, this time tweaking our strategy to include sustainability as a necessary condition, before we will truly be able to claim success as a species. Failing to do so may leave us as just another one of dozens of dead-end lines on the map of primate evolutionary history.

Contemplating the Earth's place in space, and accepting the notion that evolution here probably hasn't and won't produce highly atypical results not found elsewhere in the cosmos, the question then becomes, "What is typical? What is the common result when a higher life form achieves the intelligence to make tools and technology?" If, say, one in 1,000 exoplanets hold life like Earth, on what percentage of them will civilizations of intelligent, self-aware beings manage to achieve sustainable existences? Perhaps humanity is facing a common hurdle for life in the cosmos. Maybe developing intelligent life is easy, but perhaps it is rare for that life to not kill itself off prematurely through unsustainable living. Maybe only one of every 1,000 civilizations will achieve sustainability. Using those numbers, (one in every 1,000 exoplanets holds intelligent life, and only one of every thousand of those intelligent civilizations achieves sustainability) sustainability is literally a one-in-a-million proposition. But maybe the numbers are more generous. Maybe 50 percent of species that achieve human-level intelligence also achieve sustainability. For now, we just don't know. If we could see what else is out there, we might have some idea. If we could survey the cosmos like an angler assessing ponds from a bush plane, we might learn enough about life to know where ours is headed. Might it also serve as an incentive to get it right, an inspiration to ensure our Earth showcases the best forms and functions life has to offer rather than something far less?

Falling Apart at the Seams

There is currently a feeling of despair in America. The majority of Americans can sense it. People in general now seem willing to admit that our country and our society are in decline—headed for total collapse. Such an idea would have been unthinkable—a sacrilege—as recently as the 1990s. But now it is there, a growing notion in the minds of many. People place the blame in a variety of locations, including popular culture, TV, music, video games, moral debasement, the schools, politicians, outsourcing, financial debt, and on and on. All of these perceived ills are, directly or indirectly, elements of an unsustainable existence. It is, I believe, the unsustainability of American society that really underlies the increasing sense of despair. But if our country and our society are in decline, what will the downfall look like? What will be the symptoms of our national and societal demise?

As this chapter was being written, the mass shooting at Sandy Hook Elementary School had just occurred. A few months earlier, another mass shooting at a movie theater in Aurora, Colorado dominated the news and America's psyche. But this most recent shooting in Connecticut has especially piqued people's interest in understanding why someone would do such a thing. I believe it is, in part, one of the most grisly manifestations of societal collapse. When people give up on society, they are less apt to follow the rules that ensure society is a safe and well-ordered institution. One frequent comment about the school shootings that have plagued America for the last 20 years or so is that such a thing would never have happened in earlier times. Such a comment is absolutely right. The difference is that in earlier times, people still believed in society because the eventualities of our unsustainable lifestyle had not really begun to sink in. As our unsustainable society continues in a downward spiral, I fear we can only expect more senseless massacres. It will be one of the symptoms of a society literally coming apart at the seams.

When random acts of violence become so common that going to the mall or sending your kids to school becomes a statistically valid risk, society will further crumble because people will no longer participate in the shared activities and systems that make a society. Random violence such as mass shootings will probably coincide with targeted crime such as robbery, rape, looting, arson, home invasions and vandalism. The financial downturn of 2008-09 brought a noticeable spike in burglary and shoplifting as people feeling the financial strain committed crimes they otherwise would not have. Imagine the far greater impact a complete financial collapse, coupled with drought, famine, pandemic, and loss of organized government and social services would have. To describe the outcome as anarchy would not be hyperbole.

Just yesterday, I was pulling out of a parking lot onto a connector street. As I came to a stop before making my turn, an older lady in a stream of traffic rushing by slowed in an attempt to make a right turn into the lot I was exiting. However, she was caught up in the wave of traffic her car had become a part of and was unable to swing the turn from the point she had reached. If I had not been there, she could probably have made it, but with my car where it was, she could not cut the turn. She shot me an angry, frustrated look. My first reaction was a defensive one. "What did I do wrong? I'm right where I'm supposed to be." Then it occurred to me what was really happening. Her frustration was with the crowds and the traffic, not me. I was simply there to receive her angst.

The victims of mass shootings are in the same unenviable position I was, except with much more tragic results. Incredulity is the universal reaction to the senseless shootings that have become the norm in our society. "Why? Why would someone do it?" is the question we always ask. I believe human overpopulation is part of what's behind the decay of our society. It's part of why people are becoming more capable of mindless violence. If humans were a lot less numerous, things would be different. If instead of thousands upon thousands of anonymous faces, our daily encounters brought us into contact with only a handful of familiar people, it would be a lot less likely that unstable individuals would be inspired to mass murder. If the city streets were not choked with traffic, the woman I encountered in the parking lot would not have been radiating anger and frustration into the world around her.

Mice living in overpopulated conditions become more aggressive with one another. As humans continue to overpopulate the planet, I believe the stress that accompanies overcrowding will only result in more anti-social behavior, more mass shootings and more road rage. Imagine if rather than being fractured by the ills of an overpopulated, unsustainable existence, society came together to remake itself in the image of sustainability. Such a conversion would both inspire and refocus society, providing both a job to do and a reason to want to do it. With a renewed common purpose and real hope for the future, senseless massacres such as the Sandy Hook Elementary School shooting would again be unheard of.

Sustainability and Medicine

Since the time of Cosimo de' Medici during the renaissance, medical advances have been building a significant body of knowledge, improving and extending our lives. One of the greatest advances, from a humanitarian standpoint, has been the reduction in infant mortality rates. Medical advances have also cured many diseases, increasing the average human lifespan in the process. Every human born deserves to live a happy and healthy life, and modern medicine has made great contributions toward that end. But without a commensurate reduction in reproduction rates, this increase in survival resulting from our medical advances has caused a large and rapid increase in human population. We are seriously overpopulated, a condition that ironically threatens the future of the medical institution that made it possible.

Modern medicine relies on lots of materials (chemicals, plastics) and practices (carbon-based, resource-intensive processes and facilities) that are unsustainable. As we transition toward sustainability, we should seek to retain the medical advances we have achieved. They are among our greatest accomplishments. Finding a way to make them sustainable will require lots of "retooling." In some cases, it will be like rediscovering the advances all over again, this time in a sustainable iteration.

At times, it seems as if medicine is trying to find a way to ensure people can live forever. Medical research targets any disease, ailment or bodily failure that causes death. With what we have learned about DNA and medicine, extending human life forever no longer seems as impossibly far-fetched as it once did. Currently, most people seem to believe that there comes a point where attempting to extend life is just not worth it. When one's body is worn out, when one's time has come, letting go is the natural thing to do. There are times when the possibilities offered by modern medicine should be pursued with zeal, but there are also times when chasing a miracle by grasping at every medical possibility is folly. As medicine has advanced, the line separating the former from the latter has moved significantly. There was a time when appendicitis was a quick and mysterious killer. Now, there's no need for anyone to die from it. But the more diseases and ailments we conquer, the more we crowd the point of diminishing returns. Given enough time, medicine may relieve all the common causes of death we know today. It may even find ways to offer vitality and quality of life to people who, relieved of almost all life-threatening defects, seriously challenge the principle of senescence. Despite the fact the humans today are physically weaker and less robust that our prehistoric ancestors, we live twice as long as they did. If medicine continues on the path it has followed for the last century or two, it's easy to imagine the human lifespan doubling once again.

Embracing Sustainability

The point is, medical advances have already brought us both great improvements in health but serious problems with overpopulation. If medical advances are to continue bestowing ever greater blessings of health and longevity, we will need to deal, in earnest, with the population and sustainability challenges that come with them. We need to pay as much attention to what threatens our collective longevity as we do to our individual maladies. We need to work as hard at making our society last as we do at making our bodies last. If we don't, and when civilization hits the reset button again, as it did in 450 AD, then not only will our medical progress be halted, but many of our hard-won advances will be lost.

A Model Life

What should a sustainable lifestyle look like? How, in specific detail, should a model life of sustainability differ from the way we live now? A model life should begin in cloth diapers and end with a green burial. In between, we should live our lives modestly and in a way that shows gracious respect for the gifts our planet has to offer us. We should conserve those gifts politely, not squander them rudely. The average life of the average American—the familiar day-to-day most of us would instantly recognize as our own lifestyle—is much farther from those ideals than we realize. We are blind to our own dysfunctionality, our own unsustainability. Examining the small, mundane details of our daily routine and then considering the cumulative toll they take on the Earth's systems is a stunning reality check. Imagining ways to replace them with sustainable alternatives is a fascinating and rewarding undertaking.

Beginning the transition to a sustainable existence must start with a recognition that everything is tied to population. Our present population level will be unsustainable regardless of what we change about our lifestyles. It is only the unsustainable agricultural and industrial practices of today that have made our present overpopulation temporarily possible. There is a limit to how much human life the Earth can support at one time. Taking the population level higher than the limit is like robbing Peter to pay Paul—we will pay in the future for the excesses of today. That "payment" will come in the form of lower population levels in the future, perhaps much lower than what might otherwise have been possible had the carrying capacity not been exceeded.

So what would it take, in addition to a population level within the carrying capacity, to live sustainably? What would a "model" life look like? The truth is that, right now, some of the requirements would be very difficult for individuals to achieve because as a society, we have not made provisions for them. For instance, most people in America could not continue to live without a car or grocery store food. With no source of sustainably produced food and stuck in a lifestyle that demands a long commute to and from work (their livelihood), most Americans would face a tremendous hardship in attempting to carve out a sustainable existence without changes in society, industry and government that would offer sustainable alternatives. But the change has to start somewhere, and we, as individuals, have no choice but to try to do what we can in pursuit of sustainability. By starting with the easiest or most important changes first, we can make significant inroads toward sustainability while buying time to solve the harder challenges. There can be no doubt though, we need to solve all of the problems eventually.

Sustainability is an all-or-nothing proposition. It's not possible to be partly sustainable—a way of life is either sustainable or it is not.

Let's look at a day in a model life of sustainability and explore what it would entail and how it would be different from what the average American knows today. There are lots of small points to be addressed, but four overarching imperatives (in addition to population) cover the majority of what separates a model life from the ones we live today. Pondering these four major points is useful in understanding the core components of sustainability. They are:

1) SUSTAINABLE FOOD

    A model life would be one in which the food that sustains us is itself sustainable. That eliminates virtually all of the food that can be purchased anywhere today. Being organic or "all-natural" or non-GMO does not mean that a food is sustainably grown, harvested, processed, packaged, transported and marketed. Basically, if you buy it from a grocery store today, its continued presence as a food choice is probably not sustainable. To become sustainable, the entire food supply chain would need to be overhauled to adhere to the requirements being discussed here for a model life (that is, to begin with, zero landfill, 100 percent renewable energy powered, and no use of plastics). Given that farm equipment (tractors, combines, etc.) that runs on anything except diesel or gasoline fuel is nonexistent, truly sustainable food is currently impossible to achieve. Even if someone wanted to try to grow his or her own food using horses or oxen as a source of power to plant and harvest, try feeding those animals without hay or grain produced by petroleum-powered machines. And try finding implements for them to pull that were not manufactured using energy from fossil fuels. The scale of change necessary to achieve sustainability in the food production industry seems daunting, but if we put our hearts and minds into the job, it could probably be achieved in a generation or two. It would be an agricultural revolution we could actually be proud of!

    The truly scary fact of farming today is that regardless of anything else, organic food could never be produced on the scale necessary to feed the number of humans on Earth today. If every man, woman and child alive demanded to eat only organic food, it would be impossible to grow enough to feed them all. It's only through the unsustainable use of chemical fertilizers, herbicides and pesticides that we can be as productive as we must be to feed everyone today. Since sustainable food would absolutely need to be organic (and more), sustainable food for seven billion is an automatic non-starter. So what can we do? The answer is that, for now, we do the best we can. Grow as much of your own food as possible. Freeze, can or preserve enough homegrown grain, fruit, vegetables and meat to last until next harvest season. Save your own seed for replanting, or at least know how to do so. Of the food buying choices you have, purchase only the food that was brought into existence and put before you with the least amount of resource friction possible. Demand more sustainable choices from the food industry. When the powers that be realize the demand exists, they will seek the profits to be had by meeting it.

2) RENEWABLE ENERGY.

All the energy used for both industrial and household purposes and for transportation (and for the production and transportation of all the products we buy) must come from renewable sources. For most people in most parts of the world, that will be solar. Relying on fossil fuels in any capacity is simply not sustainable because they will eventually run out. Powering one's own life from 100 percent renewable energy is very doable if you have the money to invest in the necessary equipment. I have been fortunate enough to have done so for several years and can attest that it works. Anyone who says it won't is simply wrong. The technology is available now, and is only getting better and cheaper. But the fossil fuel industries have been using their influence to stand in the way of widespread adoption of renewable energy because it will bankrupt them (unless they change their business model and get into renewables). The more widely renewable energy is adopted, the more affordable it will become.

3) ZERO LANDFILL.

A model life generates no waste that cannot be composted, recycled or incinerated. Provided you can control what products are brought into your home and provided you have a way to incinerate part of your waste stream (either by burning it yourself or by taking it somewhere to have it done), living a zero-landfill life is really a matter of willpower. It takes dedication to religiously sort waste, but with that dedication, zero-landfill status is within anyone's grasp.

4) NO PLASTIC.

This means not buying food packaged in plastic and not buying products that are made of plastic or contain plastic-based materials. For instance, lots of clothing and furniture is made of synthetic materials that are basically plastic polymers. Many household items and most children's toys contain plastic. Common appliances such as microwave ovens, refrigerators, freezers and the like are full of unnecessary plastic. There's no reason or excuse to use plastic for any of these applications. Obviously, this "no plastic" imperative is extremely difficult if not impossible in a world where plastic-free alternatives do not exist because industry has not seen fit to provide them. As a society, we need to demand them. It's our world and our future. It ought to be our choice. Given the fact that up until the early 1900s, everyone lived plastic free lives, doing so would certainly be possible for us today.

Ingenuity is the key to ferreting out ways to circumvent the plastic lifestyle that is thrust upon us at every turn. For instance, I noticed that milk jugs accounted for a big portion of the plastic waste generated in my household. After discovering that even the half-gallon paper cartons now contain plastic spouts with plastic caps, it occurred to me that I could buy powdered milk, which comes in cardboard boxes, and mix it in a one-gallon, stainless steel milk pail. Now the milk I use generates no plastic waste whatsoever. Our recycling container no longer overflows with plastic milk jugs. There are lots of ways the average consumer can reduce his or her plastic use. With the help of industry, we could take it to zero, but that won't happen until people demand it (or until we run out of hydrocarbons from which to manufacture plastic).

Most of the plastic made and used today is unnecessary. We could easily do without it or substitute sustainable materials such as wood, metal or glass. A few applications, however, would be difficult to find ways around. Toothbrush bristles are one such example. Before plastic, toothbrushes used to be wooden handles with pig hair for bristles. (It would be interesting to see how that would go over with many of the people living today.) In addition to toothbrushes, plastic or similar synthetic materials are also used in certain medical equipment, the soles of footwear, coatings to insulate electrical wires and other applications for which wood, metal or glass-based materials would not work. For these very limited applications, plastic made from vegetable oil could be used as long as these items were strictly controlled to ensure they were recycled or incinerated. Using vegetable oil to make "bio plastic" as a substitute for all our current plastic uses would not be sustainable or wise. The vast majority of current uses for plastic are frivolous, wasteful and excessive. And plastic that doesn't get recycled or incinerated (most of it) ends up polluting our soil and water and endangering the lives of animals that will eat it. In a model life, plastic would be rare and carefully handled to ensure it did not enter the natural world, where it is a toxic, foreign material that does not belong. Bio plastic comes from vegetable oil, which must be grown, so just because it is a renewable resource doesn't mean we can produce it in unlimited quantities. If bio plastic is used for a few select applications, it must remain a choice of last resort.

Basically, a model life would need to be one that emphasized conservation and frugality over profligacy and convenience. Our priorities would need to change. There are 318 million people and 2 billion acres of land in America. That means only about 6.5 acres of land exist for every person in this country. To be sustainable, total per capita consumption of natural resources must be below the level that can be sustainably produced by that 6.5 acres of land. Remember, sustainable means not sending the biodiversity of the planet into a downward spiral or preventing other species of plant and animal life from thriving. Human use of land must yield to nature's use of the same space in as much as is necessary to ensure that nature can thrive. This does not mean we can't use any land. Clearing an acre of land to build a house and plant a garden is acceptable if the plant and animal life in the area can maintain robust, healthy populations. But at our current population levels, each of us should be balancing our resource consumption with what can be produced sustainably by 6.5 acres of land. That's impossible. But if the human population level was allowed to decline to about 70 million worldwide, it would mean a resource base of 650 acres for each of about 3 million people in America. That figure of 650 acres sounds a lot more doable than 6.5, but in reality, the exact acreage necessary to sustainably support each of us would vary according to the productivity of the land and, of course, how demanding we chose to be. Any reductions we could make in our resource consumption and waste production would proportionally increase the likelihood the 650 acres of productive Earth that exist for each one of us could support us permanently.

Americans are obsessed with cars and trucks. Many see big, fuel-guzzling vehicles as some kind of robust extension of themselves. Certain owners of pickup trucks are the worst in this regard, while SUV owners are a close second. These people could never imagine themselves driving a vehicle no more powerful or larger than necessary to accomplish necessary tasks. This attitude, which exists to varying degrees across a large swath of

American society, is a big problem. That said, it could vanish in a generation if the children of today grow up to be more reasonable and better adjusted adults than the cohort of ego-maniacs currently comprising a significant share of American car buyers.

A model life would be one that sought to minimize the resources devoted to transportation. The average American car is more than twice as large and twice as heavy as it needs to be. Car sizes and weights need to be radically rethought. Why should a car meant to carry 200-pound people weigh two tons or more? Cars no bigger or heavier than an ATV (four-wheeler) would be a great goal for engineers to pursue. Many urban Americans get by with no car. That's great, but impossible for everyone. If you need a car (or truck), it should be no larger than it has to be and should be powered by renewable energy. With current technology, that means an electric vehicle. EVs are beginning to take hold in the market, but have a tremendous amount of ground to cover to replace gasoline and diesel vehicles. This is where automobile manufacturers are going to have to step up and help out. Vehicles that run on fossil fuels have got to go the way of the horse and buggy.

A model life would involve a home considerably smaller than the average American house is now. The smaller the house, the less material goes into constructing it and the less energy is needed to heat and cool it. Keeping all these numbers as low as possible is part of being efficient and parsimonious, which goes a long way toward achieving sustainability. The same can be said of the possessions that go inside our homes. Less is better.

Keeping a smaller home uncluttered and junk-free will give you more room and make the space feel larger than if it were crammed with stuff. Breaking free from the addictive cycle of materialism will also save you a lot of money. Advertisers have cultivated the perception that to be happy, we need to be continually buying stuff. Some people joke that to them, shopping is therapeutic. What they mean is that they feel better after they acquire new possessions. It's simply not sustainable for us to acquire material items at the rate and quantity we do. It causes the amount of resources expended to support our existence to far exceed what even the target resource base of 650 acres per person could provide. Limiting material possessions does more than allow one to live in a much smaller house without clutter. It means fewer resources are directed toward supporting our existence. By owning less stuff, less industrial activity is conducted on our behalf, and less waste is generated. Reducing the scale of resource consumption at the societal level is as important as reducing our personal resource consumption. We will need to do both. The key lies in differentiating between what we need and what we merely want. We are thoroughly indoctrinated into a materialistic lifestyle that makes it difficult for us to limit our consumption to what we reasonably

Embracing Sustainability

need. Excess has become the norm. So how much is enough, and how much is too much? Trying to answer that question by asking whether a particular item has a place in your current lifestyle will not work. Instead, ask whether there's any way you could do without that item. What if you couldn't afford it or it wasn't available? What would you do then? Much of what we acquire, we acquire because we can, not because we must.

Electronics and toys present both a great challenge but also a great opportunity for reducing our material footprint. Currently, children's toys almost universally contain plastic. Most are 100 percent plastic. Go to Toys R' Us or Wal-Mart and try to find plastic-free toys for kids. It's an exercise in futility. A model life would be one in which children's toys were not plastic. It would also be one in which they were less numerous. According to The Telegraph, the average British child owns 238 toys, but plays with only about 12 favorites. Americans are even worse. According to a UCLA study, America is home to 3.1 percent of the world's children, but accounts for 40 percent of the world's toys. Loving your children (or grandchildren) does not mean you must shower them with material goods. Doing so simply indoctrinates them into a materialistic lifestyle and trains them to be over-consumptive adults. If you can't find a better way than that to express your affection, you lack both imagination and a vision for the future. Producing all these plastic toys requires both energy and physical resources. The manufacturing process also generates waste, and of course, the toys are destined to become waste themselves.

Electronic devices are present in virtually every American home. Each such device contains not only plastic but internal components made of either very toxic or very rare materials. In a model life, the plastic would be replaced with a sustainable material such as metal, glass and wood. Ensuring that the innards of our electronic devices were sustainable would involve making sure they were part of a continuous and tightly controlled recycling loop powered by renewable energy. If the average American could cut the number of electronic devices they own by half, the result would mean a lot less per-capita resource friction associated with these devices. And of course, if our population were anywhere near what it should be, the resources tied up in electronics would indeed be meager in comparison to today's situation.

A model life would need to focus on balancing the energy used in our daily activities with the amount of renewable energy generated either on site, by the home's own solar or wind capacity, or by the per-capita energy production of a local, commercial renewable energy facility. A model life would have replaced gasoline and diesel engines with electric vehicles and equipment, the energy consumption of which must also be in balance with what we produce.

We are currently energy hogs in every sense. We think nothing of making a second trip to the grocery store if we forget something or of "going out" for even the most trifling of reasons. We currently use a lot more energy than can be sustainably provided. In an energy-balanced model life, such excess would be recognized as the inefficient waste it is. We would look at our activities in a different way than we do now. We would think of them in terms of the energy expended to conduct them, which is a factor few people consider. How many kilowatt hours of energy does it take to heat your day's allotment of hot water or to power your commute to work? We would consider our energy expenditures as judiciously as we budget our monetary ones. Making sure that our energy use and the amount of renewable energy produced on our behalf are in balance is essential in a model life. The first step in achieving this balance is reducing how much energy we use. Within our homes, all energy must be renewable electric. Natural gas or fuel oil for heat is unsustainable. Geothermal heating and air is the most efficient at turning electricity into warm or cool air. A heat pump is cheaper to buy than a geothermal unit and is still more efficient than conventional electric heat. Wood is also a renewable resource, as long as it is sustainably harvested. For people who live in wooded areas and who have access to enough wood that their usage won't impact the health of the forest, high-efficiency woodstoves can be a great part of a sustainable energy portfolio.

Even though many Americans currently supplement their electric energy with petroleum-based power for heat, the average American household still uses more than 900 kilowatt hours of electricity per month. That number can be cut in half through use of efficient appliances and by not using electricity at all when it isn't needed. Hot water gushes through the pipes of American homes in obscene quantities. In a model life, hot water would be regarded as the precious commodity it is. A lot of energy is required to heat water, and it should be reserved for quick showers and frugal dishwashing. It takes 10.8 kilowatt hours of electricity to increase the temperature of 50 gallons of water by 80 degrees Fahrenheit. A 2- to 3-minute shower with a 1.25 GPM showerhead translates into about 3 gallons of hot water for a shower. That's a significant improvement over 17.2 gallons per shower, the average for Americans today, and it can be achieved with just a few modest improvements in our equipment and priorities. Hot water can be even cheaper, from both an energy and a monetary perspective, if it is generated by a heat-pump hot water heater as opposed to a conventional electric unit. The heat pump takes heat from the air to make water hot. In the summer, the cool air blown from the compressor is like free air conditioning. Even in the winter, it's cheaper than heating the water with an electric heating element. If you have "free" hot air from a wood stove burning wood from a

Embracing Sustainability

sustainable source, then even in winter, a heat pump water heater is a marvelous piece of efficiency.

If the people living in a house are willing to conserve, the average electric use of 900 kilowatt hours can be cut in half. A smaller house built with energy efficiency in mind can cut that number in half again. The average new house built in America is 2,600 square feet in size, up from 2,400 just a few years ago. That's needlessly large. It takes more to heat or cool, and a space that large invites the collection of material goods. What's the optimum sized home for someone attempting to live a sustainable life? A good rule-of-thumb is 700 to 900 square feet plus 100 to 150 square feet for each resident. Following that formula, a home for a single person might be between 800 and 950 square feet. A family of four would call 1,100 to 1,500 square feet home. The 2,000 square foot home I live in is too large, but my father lives in a 900-square-foot home and uses just under 5 kilowatt hours of electricity per day (about 150 KWH per month). The 6.5 KW photovoltaic system on his southwest facing rooftop easily produces more energy than he uses.

The modestly sized home of a model life would need to be made of sustainable materials produced and assembled in a sustainable way. Wood, stone, metal and glass can satisfy all building needs and can be produced sustainably.

Wood is a great building material. Most houses already use it for the frame and as sheathing under the roof, but wood's role can be expanded in homebuilding, especially for interior applications. To be truly sustainable, wood-based products would need to be sustainably grown and harvested locally. Also, all energy used in processing, delivering and assembling wood materials would need to be from renewable sources.

Metal and glass are also great building materials that have the potential to be sustainable. There is more than enough of each in existence to support any sustainably sized human population, and both can be recycled indefinitely. However, we currently do not manufacture or recycle metal or glass in a sustainable way. We rely on fossil fuels to generate the high temperatures necessary to melt and process metal and glass. Again, renewable energy would need to be used in all parts of the manufacturing process for the finished product to be considered truly sustainable. In addition to solar and wind, renewable sources of energy include hydro and geothermal. Heliostats can concentrate sunlight in a way that generates an amazing amount of energy. I also believe that someday, the molten interior of our planet will provide a tremendous source of energy and heat for industrial applications such as processing metal and glass.

Like wood, stone is a naturally occurring material that just needs to be harvested and cut to the right size and shape. It has been used as a building material for thousands of years and will outlast modern synthetic building materials many times over. Even brick and concrete, which are even more convenient than stone in many applications, could be made sustainably if only we perfected manufacturing processes using 100 percent renewable energy. No place does so currently, but it is a goal that could be achieved if we just had the will.

A sustainable dwelling would need to be made entirely of the aforementioned materials (sustainably produced, transported and installed wood, metal, glass, stone, brick or concrete). Sticking with these materials would eliminate several unsustainable building products commonly found in most American homes. Vinyl siding and asphalt roofing shingles are absolutely horrible building materials. They truly showcase a mentality that is blind to the future. Both are made of oil and require a lot of energy to produce. They can be recycled, but rarely are and when thrown into a landfill, constitute very unnatural materials. Wood siding and shingles would be the easiest materials to produce sustainably, but they are short-lived. Metal siding and roofing is a much better material, and would only need to be manufactured using renewable energy to be 100 percent sustainable. As this chapter is being written, metal roofs are beginning to gain popularity quickly, mostly because they are becoming cheaper than asphalt shingles.

Rigid foam insulation is the worst possible choice of thermal barrier. Fiberglass insulation, being made of glass, is somewhat better, but as far as I know, it is never recycled and takes a lot of energy to produce. Far better, and truly sustainable, is "cellulose" insulation made of recycled paper such as that marketed under the Green Fiber name. I have personally used it in both the walls and attic of a home, and can attest that it is phenomenally good insulation that is both better for the Earth and cheaper than fiberglass insulation. The manufacturer of Green Fiber claims that the product requires only 10 percent of the energy necessary to produce fiberglass insulation. That makes sense given that it's basically shredded phone books treated with a non-toxic fire retardant. The only complaints I have with this product are that it comes packaged in plastic and is likely not produced using renewable energy. Insulation is an essential building material. It is, itself, an energy saving material, so knowing that it can be sustainably produced is wonderful news. Truly sustainable insulation is within easy striking distance. The cellulose insulation currently available in every Lowes and Home Depot store is not far from being sustainable now.

Carpet, even the "green" or "eco-friendly" varieties, are not good choices. In addition to being made of synthetic, fossil-fuel based materials, carpet doesn't last nearly as long as concrete, tile or wood flooring. After it's worn out, it is usually discarded in a landfill. And as long as carpet remains in a house, it requires constant sweeping with an electric vacuum cleaner and occasional cleaning with a Rug Doctor type machine, which is also electric and uses hot water and soap. All of this sweeping and cleaning means carpet continues to require energy and resources as long as it is in use. A wood, stone or concrete floor, however, requires only a broom and a mop to maintain, and it will usually last as long as the entire house. If it ever does need replacing, wood or stone is much less detrimental as waste than used carpet. Wood can be burned for fuel, recycled into paper fiber or composted for fertilizer. Stone can be recycled or reused in a variety of ways and remains a natural material that introduces nothing unnatural or artificial no matter how it is discarded. Many Americans living in 2014 would complain vociferously at the notion of living without plush carpeting in their home. The idea of hard wood or stone flooring throughout their entire house would strike them as a terrible burden. To me, such a reaction is evidence of how spoiled many people are by the level of luxury and convenience that has become the norm. Sacrificing such excessive luxury should be a small price to pay for a sustainable existence. That said, one problem with hard floors, especially concrete, is children. They will run, and they will fall while playing. Sometimes, these falls result in them hitting their heads on the floor. A hard fall on padded carpeting is one thing, but a hard blow to the head on concrete can be disastrous. I believe we are capable of finding sustainable ways to address this problem. A home with young children could be equipped with sustainable organic cotton carpeting of a kind that could be picked up for manual cleaning. With ingenuity, even better alternatives could be devised.

Drywall is basically natural, being made of gypsum, but gypsum must be mined and then processed in a way that demands lots of energy. The same can be said of cement, but drywall is seldom as permanent as other stone-based materials like brick and concrete. Also, brick, stone and concrete can be recycled, but I'm unaware of any processes for recycling drywall. As anyone who has ever removed and disposed of drywall can attest, it creates a lot of ugly waste that invariably ends up in a landfill. Wood paneling is considerably better than drywall as a material for walls and ceilings. If sustainably sourced, processed, transported and disposed of, we could count on wood indefinitely as a surface material for interior walls and ceilings. To be truly sustainable, wood paneling would need to be made with all-natural, sustainably produced bonding agents that would not leach toxins if composted. Wood can be finished in a variety of textures and can be stained or painted any color. A natural finish is the least resource intensive. Wood's superiority over drywall becomes even clearer at the time of removal and disposal. Drywall is a nightmare to remove. It is difficult to take down, makes an incredible mess and can rarely be recycled because facilities don't exist in most areas. Wood paneling, whether attached with screws or nails, is easier to take down, comes off in one piece with no dust or mess and can be disposed of in a variety of ways that do not involve a landfill (recycling, burning or composting).

Plumbing needs a sustainable makeover as well. Pressurized water lines should be steel or copper. Drain pipes less than three inches in diameter should be aluminum or steel while trunk lines and sewer pipes four inches or larger should be vitrified clay. My local public service district will not connect clay pipes to the sewer service. They will only connect schedule 40 PVC (polyvinyl chloride). Any such regulations that prohibit sustainable choices should be struck down. It's intolerable and inexcusable that unsustainable practices are forced upon people. In the case of PVC-only sewer hook-ups, that's all the more reason to have a septic tank instead. Modern sewer systems and the accompanying water treatment facilities are seen as better choices than septic tanks. In some ways they are, especially in urban areas. But if only sustainable, chemically benign substances are used in the home, the waste water from that home can be disposed of in a septic tank with no detrimental consequences.

Cleaning dishes and household surfaces, doing laundry and bathing should proceed without the harsh, heavily scented chemicals so widely used today. Mild dish soap such as that manufactured by the Seventh Generation company works fine for dishes (even in a dishwasher), laundry (yes, laundry), mopping, as hand soap and for bathing. What you just heard me say is that all-natural, hypo-allergenic soap can be used for any cleaning need you have. Will it work as well as other substances on the market? No, it won't. But it will work well enough. You might be surprised how well. And the wastewater left after using such a benign product is nothing you would be afraid to have enter the watershed that grows your food and provides your drinking water. The toxic array of cleaning products that jam the aisles of most grocery stores are completely unnecessary. Most are the result of marketing departments trying to tease more money out of consumers' pockets. It works, but the result isn't just wasted money. The resources, plastic and pollution associated with the production and use of these products is neither frugal nor efficient.

Sewer services require lots of energy to transport and treat wastewater. Anyone trying to prepare for a sustainable existence in the face of an uncertain future should not count on such services to continue in perpetuity. Many cities are already finding it increasingly difficult to maintain the aging water and sewer lines originally installed under their streets nearly 100 years ago. These unwieldy systems are beginning to fail all at once, and the massive replacement project necessary to keep them operating is something no one can afford. The cost of doing nothing is not an option either. Significant amounts of water are lost to leaking underground pipes already. The monetary cost of this waste is something utilities have to either absorb or pass along to their customers. In places where water is scarce, leaking pipes waste important resources. The problem will only continue to get worse until, eventually, the system becomes untenable. It's a small-scale case study in sustainability. Despite being easily predictable, no one bothered to think about our current predicament when the system of water lines was being built. No one bothered to think about it during the intervening decades either. But now that a serious problem is coming home to roost, people are both surprised and worried about this "new" problem now facing them. Our problems maintaining an unsustainable system of water lines is not unique. Every aspect of our modern lifestyles is unsustainable, and eventually, every one of them will come crashing down on us. The wise course of action would be to find better ways, sustainable ways, while there's still time.

  A model life would include a well or a spring as a water source and a septic tank for processing waste. If that isn't how you're doing it now, then you're not living sustainably. When coal mining operations cause wells and springs to go dry, their answer is to bring water in, by truck if necessary, to "mitigate" the loss. It is only when someone truly understands how irreplaceably important wells and springs are as the only sustainable sources of water that the tragic absurdity of the "pipe it in or truck it in" mentality comes into focus. The errant belief of the coal industry was that the coal was more valuable than the wells and springs destroyed in the mining process. If necessary, they would compensate people's water loss, but nothing could be allowed to stand in the way of extracting the coal. In reality, this misguided belief system was wrong on every level. The people who made those decisions sacrificed our water resources forever in exchange for a very short-term supply of dirty energy that could have been had in other ways. It's hard to imagine a worse deal. The loss of water will remain long after the energy from the coal has been used up, reminding us how foolish the trade was. And when we discover that we can't replace the lost wells and springs with tanks and pipes forever, the true value of sustainable water sources will become painfully clear.

  A model life would involve considering the lawn and landscaping surrounding one's home in terms of sustainability as well. Non-native vegetation adds nothing and is sometimes detrimental to biodiversity, and grass that requires maintenance such as mowing or watering takes a sizeable toll in natural resources. Native vegetation should be allowed to grow naturally on all but a small area immediately surrounding the home. An expansive, trophy lawn whose purpose is to impress the neighbors actually showcases only the misguided priorities of the property owner. If he or she has the resources to maintain a lawn of that type, he or she should channel them into conservation, not waste. A low-cut, comfortable place for kids to play is the best reason for wanting a lawn, and for that purpose, a small yard of half an acre or less is enough. Kids can always explore beyond the manicured boundaries if they want, or stay in the short grass is they wish. The purpose of mowing should be mainly to keep tall grass and weeds at bay in a small select area near the house. The best response to drought or the late-summer dry months when vegetation doesn't grow should be none at all. A lawn that is brown is one that won't need mowing in the foreseeable future, which is a good thing. Watering to keep a lawn green is vain and wasteful, and should be avoided along with fertilizer or chemical treatments. Suburban America's chemical warfare against dandelions is another example of a culture with the wrong priorities and no understanding of the natural world or land ethic.

Something unsustainable, by definition, cannot be maintained. Therefore, our current lifestyle, which is unsustainable in almost every way, will not last. We got where we are today by proceeding without a plan. When making choices and developing new ways of living, we focused on the present or the short term rather than on the long-term viability of our decisions. Human civilization and modern societies developed by doing whatever provided a favorable result in the moment. Convenience and instant gratification were the criteria used to select how we would do things. We allowed industry, which is motivated to do only what is profitable, to chart the course for much of our development as a society. By failing to consider the future, we have ensured that we will start running into all kinds of problems when that future finally arrives. We will find that the lifestyle, policies and practices we thought were fine are plagued with fatal flaws.

If we do not start striving for and embracing true sustainability, the unavoidable demise of our current lifestyle will be a tremendous hardship. The change will be harsh and abrupt. Most people will be completely unprepared, and it's likely we will have neither the time nor the means to adapt to a radically different set of living conditions when they suddenly arise. If, however, we begin preparing while there is still time, we can approach the process of adopting sustainable practices in a systematic way. We will hopefully have time to identify unsustainable aspects of our lives and our society, investigate sustainable alternatives and test the new ways. Reinventing our lifestyle from the ground up is bound to include some unforeseen complications. It would be nice to have time to deal with them and sort out what works from what doesn't, the easy and efficient from the difficult. Fine tuning a sustainable existence would be a much more pleasant task if conducted before the unsustainable existence it is meant to replace collapses.

Our lives are not about us. They are about the future. Although we should never live in a way that puts our interests ahead of those of future generations, most of us do. It's time to remake our lives and our society to be what they should have been all along—sustainable. Anything less is to accept defeat and sacrifice the future for no good reason.

None Quicker Than Ours

I just heard a news story that more than 100 million sharks are killed every year by commercial fishing operations. That's 11,000 every hour, 24-7-365. The report indicated that such loss was unsustainable because shark reproduction rates can't keep up with that level of loss. Sharks and rays have lower reproduction rates than other fish in part because they are slow to change as a species. They evolved with the dinosaurs and have occupied a very stable, slow-to-change niche for hundreds of millions of years. But now, 25 percent of all shark species are in danger of extinction because of a huge spike in mortality rates that began when we humans started intensive commercial fishing a few decades ago. The news report ended by saying that conservation efforts could help many shark and ray species avoid extinction, but that without such efforts, many of these species were "quickly heading for oblivion." My first reaction to that statement was the title of this essay: None quicker than ours. It's ironic that we can recognize the warning signs of extinction in sharks and rays but can't see that the same forces threatening them—our unsustainable lifestyles and practices—will also be our own undoing.

Unnatural

If the behavior of human beings could be observed alongside that of other animals from afar, one of the most notable observations would be how unnatural and unhealthy many of our actions are. I'm not speaking just of the things we do that harm the planet, but rather the things we do that destroy ourselves. The percentage of people who smoke cigarettes is unfathomable. Who would do such a thing? The whole process is so weird, it would be hard to imagine if it weren't reality. Think about it. A large and complex tobacco industry makes billions of dollars from millions of people who willingly pay money to inhale toxic smoke. Everyone knows it's bad for them, but many just don't care. What other animal does such a thing? None. Every animal I know of is endowed with an instinct to avoid smoke, probably because it usually indicates the presence of fire. None would breathe it if given a choice. First time smokers cough and get sick from cigarette smoke, but they intentionally keep at it until their bodies' natural defenses are worn down and replaced by the cravings of addiction. What kind of being would do such a thing? What kind of logic or values underlie such a decision? And that's just cigarettes. We also have alcoholics, people addicted to all kinds of legal and illegal drugs, people with eating disorders as well as people who just misuse food by gorging themselves with all kinds of unsuitable junk until they're fat and sick. Human beings are exceedingly strange. In fact, many common human behaviors are completely unnatural. No other animal does these things. Animals eat what nature intended and avoid things that would make them sick. No wild animals ever end up with the addictions or disorders that are commonplace in humans. It should come as no surprise that a being so prone to self-destructive, unnatural behavior would also be prone to abusing the life-giving resources of the planet on which it depends. If people don't even care about their own bodies, what is the likelihood they will be good stewards of the planet? And if they aren't likely to take good care of the Earth, why are they entitled to make decisions regarding it?

Ungrateful

Everything about our existence is a graceful gift of chance and perhaps providence. Our planet's ability to sustain life as it does is a miraculous convergence of factors including the size and placement of our sun, our moon and the other planets in our solar system, not to mention myriad smaller but equally important details about our planet's mass, age, atmosphere, axis and oceans. If any of these elegant details were awry, we wouldn't be here. But instead of appreciating the greatness of our circumstance, we are insolent.

Yesterday was Earth Day. I came into contact with at least 100 people throughout the course of the day, but I didn't hear a single sincere salutation recognizing the holiday. I did, however, hear three sarcastic comments from people satirizing the day and what it stands for. Earth Day seems to have become a politicized holiday—perhaps the only holiday that it is not taboo to disrespect. Ridiculing religious holidays will be perceived as hateful intolerance. Even patriotic holidays like the Fourth of July, Memorial Day, President's Day and certainly Veterans Day are safe from mean-spirited sarcasm. But not Earth Day.

With the exception of the huge garbage patch floating in the middle of the Pacific Ocean, the line between uninhabited wilderness and areas frequented by humans can be delineated clearly by trash. Everywhere people go, you will, without exception, find trash. Usually, the degree of human presence correlates with the amount of trash to be found.

One need look no further than the nearest roadside to find irrefutable evidence that, generally speaking, humans don't give a damn about this planet. People's willingness to toss whatever they want out the window of their speeding cars is testament to their cavalier disrespect of the green jewel that gives us life. Of course, we do a lot of things that bring greater harm than littering. The forces of industry are raping this planet, and we, with our collective purchasing decisions, are bankrolling their carnage. But few actions illustrate our throwaway attitude toward the Earth as clearly and simply as the insult of our litter. Real idiots who dump truckloads of tires, toilets, couches, refrigerators and similar junk over steep hillsides corroborate beyond a doubt the indictments presented by our capricious litter. Like the criminals they are, they sneak through the night to perpetrate their harm unseen. Once they've tossed their loads, they race off like cowards.

Most, maybe all, of our unsustainable practices can be assailed on the grounds that if we don't correct them, future generations will suffer direct harm. But there should also be an element of gracious respect for the Earth involved. We speak often of respecting human dignity. Philosophers and ethicists speak of the moral high ground we take when we decide to do the right thing, even when we don't have to. We think highly of people whose conscience and inner compass make them totally honest and utterly trustworthy. But when it comes to taking care of the Earth, we are not as quick to recognize right for right's sake. We don't see the same intrinsic value in the natural world that we recognize in other arenas. Any grievance regarding crimes against nature must be expressed in some tangible metric, usually monetary damages or human health, before any relief will be offered. To say that a mountain should be preserved because it is ancient or beautiful or sacred is insufficient in a culture that does not share those values. Courts and governmental regulatory agencies are terrible about this. Some of the most heinous assaults against our planet cannot be argued directly, for the worst things about them won't matter to those in authority.

    The reason for all of this is that people don't respect the Earth. They don't revere it. They are not humbled by the glorious gift of life (their own and that of everything else in the biosphere) that exists only by sweet chance. Maybe they're just ignorant, or maybe they really don't care. Whatever the cause, the takeaway is that far too often, people are ungrateful for the Earth, and that is a big problem.

Unqualified

By participating in society, humans collectively decide how the Earth's resources will be used. That includes how we get energy, what we manufacture, how we use and dispose of those items, as well as how the land is impacted by our activities. The average American consumer influences, through purchasing decisions, how industries impact the Earth. The average American voter decides who will hold elected positions and affect laws and regulations regarding use of the Earth's resources. But the average American is unqualified to make such decisions and unqualified to select a proxy to make them on his or her behalf.

Most Americans wouldn't know the difference between tree of heaven and white oak. As managers of the Earth's natural resources, they are incompetent, utterly inept. They have no understanding of how complex ecosystems function and no appreciation of the diverse team of plant and animal life that composes them. Most Americans wouldn't know the difference between a starling and a cerulean warbler. They would probably see them as equally valuable, if they perceived any value at all. Most Americans wouldn't know the difference between brook trout and grass carp, between crown vetch and fire pink, between a Cadiz fly and a gypsy moth. This mentality is at the heart of believing a reclaimed strip mine looks good or thinking that bulldozing 100 acres of hardwood forest for a shopping mall is a smart development of "unused" land. Allowing such ignorance to decide the fate of our planet is as unthinkable as allowing a random passenger to fly a commercial jetliner or asking an illiterate person to select the next poet laureate (or more accurately, to decide whether we have literature at all). The average American is unqualified to be steward of the planet on which we live because most people have no idea what sustainability is, why we must achieve it or how to do so.

Why Not Always?

It's February 2014, and I've just been reading some news stories on the unprecedented drought in California. People being interviewed, even old ones, say they've never experienced anything like it before. Snowpack in the mountains is said to be 12 percent of average. Reservoirs are within a few weeks of going dry. A study of tree rings suggests the last 12 months have been the driest in more than 500 years. The situation is an uncontested emergency, and people affected by it seem genuinely scared. Many of the news reports are detailing measures being taken to conserve water. Municipalities have banned watering lawns and washing cars. Some water utilities are knocking on doors of heavy users asking them directly to reduce consumption. Restaurants are serving water only on request now. Individuals are taking a variety of measures, including flushing toilets only when absolutely necessary, cutting down on laundry and showering less often. In short, they are sacrificing luxury and convenience for conservation. That's a notion that offends some people. Suggesting that our normal lifestyles are wasteful elicits a visceral response of defensive indignation.

It's likely that some people who are now conserving water in drought-ravaged California would have reacted to the notion of conservation in just such an indignant way prior to the emergency. Why does it take a disaster to make conservation seem sensible? Why are efficiency and stewardship not foremost in people's minds at all times? I pose that as a sincere question. I really don't understand. I like being comfortable, but I do not find striving for efficiency and conservation to be uncomfortable. I do not find attempts to use as little as possible at odds in any way with good living. In fact, the shame of excess is what I find uncomfortable.

Better Days

There was a time when our ancestors worshipped the sun as a god and gave heartfelt thanks for the coming and going of the seasons. They weren't as knowledgeable or sophisticated as we are, but they were grateful for everything that made life possible. We know better than they did why the seasons change as they do. We have computer models that can predict the weather with a detached precision, but we seem to detest the seasons. We complain if it rains and complain if it doesn't. We curse the cold and bemoan the heat. Despite living on a planet that has beaten great odds to find itself in a sweet-spot "Goldilocks zone" that allows the splendor of life to bloom, people's everyday comments about the weather are predominantly negative. How insolent. We should be awestruck with gratitude for the elegant climate we have inherited. After all, we know more of the details of its intricate clockwork than any of our ancestors ever did but seem to have the least appreciation.

When the next ice age advances, much of our country will be locked in what will seem eternal winter. In the meantime, as we overload our atmosphere with carbon, heat and drought may roast areas that were previously mild and temperate. But for now, we remain locked in a tenuous dance where winter, spring, summer and fall complete a stable cycle every year and rain falls in predictable amounts. Why is it too much to ask that we display the appreciation and humble reverence such a system deserves?

Rare Earth, Precious Earth

I never cease to be amazed by the miracle of life on Earth. People almost always take it for granted because humanity developed here. If humans were to come to a planet like Earth from somewhere else, like sci-fi plots often suggest, we would have a much different worldview with much more respect and conservation ethic. We are like teenagers who, having lived their whole lives in their parents' house, take it for granted. When such teenagers grow up and get a place of their own, they generally take better care of it and respect it more. Despite the dreams of some, we will never be able to move on to a new home (planet). Humans will always be bound to the Earth. If we could see our existence here as the miracle it is, we could begin to live in a way that didn't reek of brash arrogance and unbridled ignorance.

Have you ever watched a child blowing bubbles on a sunny afternoon and seen a single, rather lucky bubble that persists long after most others have burst? It will float along on the wind, narrowly avoiding the ground and seeming to rebuff the drying effect of the sun. After noticing the one bubble that outlived all the rest, it is impossible to take your eyes off it because you know that the longer it lasts, the more likely the moment of its impending doom is at hand. In some ways, we want to see the bubble that has managed to outlast its peers last as long as possible. The longer it remains, the more disappointing its eventual demise seems. The life that currently flourishes on Earth is as fragile a miracle as any bubble ever blown. The Earth itself is a chunk of iron and rock floating through the harshness of space, but the thin layer of life coating its surface is an amazing and precious turn of events. The biosphere of Earth is just as fleeting and vulnerable as a child's bubble. Let conditions change even a little, and the Earth would be a much different (lifeless) place. The difference between our planet's current state and that of our closest neighbors Mars and Venus is about the same as the difference between the bubble that lasts and those that perished. The random confluence of certain variables along with a lot of luck serve as the foundation of our own existence. Very few people understand or appreciate that. Those who do see life differently. They revere and cherish the Earth. Their every instinct is to protect and preserve it because they are keenly aware that it is delicate and that all life depends on its continued well-being.

Some cultures, particularly ancient ones, worshipped the sun and the Earth. Some had Earth-gods or gods to whom they ascribed the changing seasons. Today, we tend to view such belief systems as primitive. We might say, "Those ancient people did not understand the natural world the way we do today. They didn't have our scientific understanding, and so they feared and thus worshipped the mysterious things they could not explain." Perhaps that's true, but in some ways their thinking benefitted from an appreciation of the Earth most people lack today. If understanding is defined as the ability to explain, with scientific accuracy, how something works, then yes, we have superior understanding. But what those ancient cultures seemed to have that modern society lacks is a reverence and appreciation of the Earth. If I could have only one, I would take the latter (appreciation) over the former (understanding) any day.

Recycled Mistakes

The current push for recycling is evidence that our society is very far from a sustainable state of existence, so far in fact that most people cannot even comprehend how deeply flawed our current systems are. Recycling plastic milk jugs, detergent containers, pop bottles, yogurt cups and other junk is not a happy solution that makes right all the ills associated with throwing such material into a landfill.

Plastic lasts a very long time, but can only be recycled a few times. After that, the only options for disposal are to throw it away, incinerate it or convert it back into oil (which is what it's made from). A company from Buffalo, New York known as Plastic To Oil specializes in this process. Almost any kind of plastic, clean or dirty, can be reduced to the equivalent of crude oil using this company's process. This oil is molecularly identical to the oil that companies like Chevron and BP pump out of the ground and can be used for all the same purposes. Oil made (remade) from plastic releases the same amount of CO_2 when it's burned, but at least doing so finally eliminates the plastic from which it was derived.

Very little of the world's plastic is disposed of through Plastic To Oil's process. The vast majority ends up in the ground, in our waterways and in the ocean. Where else can it go? It is in these places that it begins to disintegrate (not decompose, there is a big difference) and to enter the food chain as animals of all kinds (vertebrates and invertebrates) begin to eat it. Many will die from having a gut full of plastic chips. Recycling plastic is definitely better than not, because it saves energy (less is required to recycle plastic than to create new) and temporarily slows the amount of new plastic manufactured. But recycling plastic does not make it OK for us to produce and use it because recycling cannot permanently keep plastic out of the ground and water. That we produce all this unnatural plastic stuff is evidence that we, as a society, are shortsighted, selfish fools who care only about convenience, profit and eye-appeal.

The food packaging and delivery systems in modern societies are a tragedy. We package food in small plastic containers because it's cheap and easy and it maximizes profits. Nobody, at least nobody in a position to affect the practice, seems to care. How can people be so blind as to not notice or care that our food packaging is not sustainable? Packaging everything in plain, unbleached paper, cardboard (waxed if necessary to prevent wet items from leaking or to preserve freshness), metal or glass would allow all waste to be disposed of sustainably. Recycling all materials that can be recycled is our duty, and that duty should not be subject to the economics of the process. Some places balk at recycling glass because there is no financial advantage in doing so. It is this boneheaded focus on only what is profitable that has gotten us into the unsustainable mess we're currently facing. Such an attitude should no longer be permitted to win the day. Corporate decision makers would scoff at the notion of eliminating plastic. They would call it "impractical." But it's impractical only if selfishness, greed and laziness are the priorities guiding the choice. Our current plastic, throw-away society is what's impractical, and recycling does not change that.

Better by Design

While picking up after a recent wind storm, it occurred to me how obtuse and ill-designed our build environment is compared to the highly evolved and synchronous natural world. Structures built by humans (houses, signs, fences, etc.) always seem to suffer the most damage from storms. Yes, trees often blow down. They all do eventually, but pay attention to which ones succumb to severe wind storms. It's usually either the weak or dying specimens or the ones we have planted in a spot they would not have naturally grown. Far more frequently, the wind merely helps provide some natural pruning by breaking off a limb here or there. The forest has evolved in the presence of regular wind events and is supremely well-adapted and prepared to deal with them. Wind and storms are really a problem only for us and our infrastructure. The lesson to take from this is that we humans, especially in our modern form, are relative newcomers trying to exist in a system to which we are not attuned. We could learn a lot about longevity and sustainability by taking philosophical notice of how natural systems work.

Natural systems have worked out all the kinks and smoothed out all the rough spots. They hum along flawlessly and efficiently and seem to generate virtually no resource friction as they mesh seamlessly into everything with which they interact. Our creations, like us, are obtuse elements in a smooth, rounded world. Our lifestyles catch tremendous resistance as they jam their way through a world they don't fit. The calamitous damage human systems often incur from wind storms is like a metaphor for how vulnerable we are to challenges for which nature has a better design—sustainability.

Why Now, Why Us?

    Human intelligence and ingenuity, although limited, is amazing. Nothing like it has existed on the Earth before. The Earth has been a habitable place supporting life for hundreds of millions of years, but not before the last few thousand has intelligence on the scale we possess been tried. Why not? Why have no animals developed intelligence the way we did? Intelligence has proved to be a tremendously beneficial trait for us. It has propelled us almost instantly into our current position. Why would it not have been equally successful for countless other species? There seems to have been nothing standing in the way of its development millions of years ago. Evolution has been producing elegant, highly developed forms and structures in animals for a long time. Why only recently did intelligence such as ours arise? I suppose success, in evolutionary terms, was easier and quicker to achieve by other means. Perhaps in our competition with our hominid ancestors, the typical evolutionary route of physical adaptations were not paying off by offering a significant advantage over our competitors. But again, had other life forms not been in similar evolutionary struggles with closely related lines of competitors before? I've heard the theories of how climate stability played a role in the emergence of humans, but again, surely there were other lengthy periods with a stable climate in the history of life on Earth.

    I consider it pretty far-fetched to think that human-level intelligence existed at any point before us. There is no evidence of it in the fossil record. But it's equally hard to comprehend why it didn't. It seems impossible that an animal could develop intelligence equal to our own and not follow the same tool-making, industrial path we did. But is it? Could an animal be as intelligent as us but still live like other animals? What, then, would be the outlet for such intelligence, such creativity? Surely such intelligence would manifest in clear and unmistakable ways.

    We consider our intelligence to be the top of the scale because it bests any other animal on the planet, but clearly there is headroom above our own level. What would intelligence greater, perhaps much greater, than our own look like? The intelligence gap between us and an opossum seems incomprehensible. Our intelligence is not just higher, it's different. We don't just think better than an opossum, we think differently. Our greater intelligence has opened to us mental capacities an opossum simply doesn't possess, at any level. So it's not just that our mental function is higher or farther along some continuum, it is in many ways not even on the same line. And speaking of lines, does intelligence increase linearly, or does it follow a logarithmic or even exponential scale as many other natural phenomena do? If you consider the intelligence gap between us and an opossum, and then jump beyond our own level by that same amount, where does that put you? How might the mind of a being that much beyond our own intelligence function? What would such a being be aware of that we are blind to? I once heard the famous scientist David Suzuki describe intelligence as the ability to predict the future by correctly interpreting the truth about the present. Differentiating sustainable and unsustainable practices certainly involves seeing the future, but it also involves being willing to admit what that future will be. It involves being motivated enough to move past apathy, denial and fatalism. It involves the courage and character to care about that future when it might seem easier not to. It is those things, more so than intelligence, that seem to be standing between us and sustainability.

And while intelligence has definitely been key to our current success as a species, we should not forget that intelligence is not a necessary ingredient for success—adaptability is. Many of the most successful life forms on Earth, including bacteria, possess no measurable intelligence. So ultra-high intelligence, far beyond our own, would seem to be a fantastic gift, but it would not automatically guarantee success. That said, it's hard to imagine a species that intelligent that would not make the necessary accommodations to ensure its continued survival.

So why has intelligence equal to (or greater than) our own not evolved on Earth before us when it seems as though there was ample time and opportunity for it to do so? I don't know. Perhaps evolution and the random time clock it runs by simply hadn't gone there yet. An even better reason may be that the opportunity cost of acquiring that intelligence was so high as to make the trade a hard deal to strike. You see, getting smart was an offer that came with quite a few strings attached. Nearly as soon as we acquired the intelligence to make our lives significantly more comfortable than those of other animals, we lost the ability to live without those comforts. Our pre-human ancestors had the skills and abilities to live sustainably. We clearly do not. Making the jump from our pre-human "animal-like" subsistence lifestyle to the more comfortable "civilized" lifestyle of modern humans (this civilized comfort has been increasing pretty much continually for thousands of years) came at a cost. To gain comfort we gave up our ability to survive well without those comforts as our ancestors did. Proof of this can be seen everywhere. Recently, I've been watching a television show called "Naked and Afraid." In many ways, it's just another reality show that's probably scripted to ensure plenty of drama for the cameras, but it drives home a greater truth about humanity that supports my point about the costly tradeoff we made when we swapped survivability for intelligence.

In "Naked and Afraid," two people (one man and one woman) with proven survival skills and good fitness are dropped off naked and without supplies in some remote tropical wilderness, where they must survive for 21

Embracing Sustainability

days by living off the land. Needless to say, it's quite a struggle, which seems to be the point of the show. Living in the wilderness for even three weeks without the trappings of human civilization is an extreme challenge even for the experienced contestants casted for the show. The many animals living in and around the contestants' campsite, of course, have no problem existing in the jungle with nothing but what nature provides. But for the humans, just surviving for three weeks is a major accomplishment. Most are malnourished, dehydrated, fatigued and sick when they crawl out to await rescue. Watching them struggle and deteriorate during the three-week period is like watching an animal completely out of its element. But the tropics are where we cut our teeth as a species. It's warm there, with plenty of water. It's the most verdant place on Earth and, generally, life flourishes there as it does nowhere else. But even in a place like that, humans can barely survive for three weeks.

The Earth is our home. It's where we're from, but if you take away our artificial life support systems (the trappings of civilization), we may as well be on Mars, unable to survive in an inhospitable world to which we are not properly adapted to live. The answer is not in trying to recapture the survival abilities of our pre-human ancestors, but rather in finding ways to ensure the elements of civilization we require can be sustainably produced.

So perhaps the reason intelligence such as ours has never before emerged from the crucible of evolution is that the tradeoffs that inevitably accompany it always outweighed the benefits. Like trying to light a fire from damp tinder, it took a long time and a little luck before the spark of intelligence took hold and began to increase beyond the threshold found in animals such as the crow, octopus, whale, dolphin, elephant and yes, primates. Perhaps the laws of nature include some kind of a natural limit for intelligence, a glass ceiling for smarts. The limit might be found at some point just below the threshold necessary for the type of tool making and technological pursuit that so obviously separate us from the rest of the animal kingdom. Any species could evolve in such a way as to break through that glass ceiling for intelligence, but they would do so at their own risk. Through some combination of luck and circumstance, we humans seem to have taken it farther than any species before us.

Perhaps any species that breaks the glass ceiling on intelligence has some limited window of time to also incorporate sustainability into its new lifestyle. Failure to do so turns its new "civilized" lifestyle from a blessing into a curse, from a key to survival to a ticket of doom. If that's true, now is our moment of truth, our chance to make it work or suffer an epic failure. Maybe in the future, evolution will treat some species to a gift of intelligence far greater than anything we can imagine.

I guess the takeaway from pondering this mystery is that the story of life on Earth is more complicated than we know. If we cannot understand the past, we certainly cannot predict the future. We are both great and small at the same time.

What Remains

What most people seem unable to comprehend is that the natural world—those parts of the world that have been unaltered by humans—must remain that way if our planet is to continue producing the conditions that all living things, ourselves included, depend upon. You see, the things humans create may be convenient and even comfortable, but they are not life-giving. Only nature can make that stuff. The more of our planet we convert into an unnatural state, the more essential it is that the remaining natural areas are preserved. We have long since passed the point at which land use such as mountaintop removal mining can be or should be tolerated. The reclamation process that follows surface mining is completely inadequate. It does not reproduce the conditions as they were before mining. Instead, what results is a strange and barren landscape of non-native or invasive species. There is far less diversity of life on reclaimed sites, and the most important species of plants and animals—those essential to the composition of the native ecosystem—will never be found on these sites again. This is a problem. Whether people can understand it or not does not change the fact that it is a huge problem.

One of the main problems with reclaimed strip mines is the poor quality of the soil that ends up on the top after the surface has been re-graded. The rich topsoil that had been fomented over eons—topsoil full of essential minerals, nutrients and microbes and of an exact PH that many dozens of plant species evolved to depend upon—is replaced with a rocky mix of clay, shale and sandstone in which nothing of value can thrive. The conditions on a reclaimed mountaintop removal mining site are worlds apart from what had been there before and are only slightly better than a gravel pit. If you don't believe that's true or think it doesn't matter, just try planting a garden on reclaimed strip mine land. Nothing can grow well in the junk soil that remains, certainly not the delicate and finicky flora that is the foundation of an Appalachian forest ecosystem. Many species of plants and animals that can be found on Earth require very specific conditions. Without those specific conditions, these sensitive species will vanish, reducing the overall biodiversity of the planet as they go.

Strip mines are certainly not the only human practices that have the consequence of literally making the earth a smaller place by reducing the amount of natural, properly functioning land that remains. Every day, startling amounts of the natural world are subjugated into elements of the Anthropocene.

Economists tell us that as supply goes down, price goes up. As the amount of unspoiled Earth continues to decrease, what remains becomes increasingly valuable. To those who can see the clear difference between the natural world and the aftermath of human infrastructure, the sense of loss is palpable, and the urgency of protecting what remains is tangible.

If humans are hell bent on transforming the Earth into a world unsuitable for the many species of plants and animals that require very specific conditions that only nature can create (or recreate), then we are also sowing the seeds of our own destruction. You see, we are not one of the highly adapted species that can live in almost any conditions. Without our technology and conveniences, we are one of the species least-equipped to survive on Earth. If we do not pay due diligence to sustainability now, we humans will not be part of what remains when the future arrives.

Toilet Paper

    Sometimes, little things can be the most revealing. One very telling detail of our society is the fact that most people would not buy or use toilet paper made of recycled material. Marketing research has shown that most people would hesitate to do so because they feel that somehow using recycled paper would be undesirable or might result in harm. Some even believe that "recycled" toilet paper is made from used toilet paper that someone decided to recycle instead of flush. To them, it's the same as reusing soiled toilet paper. The aversion is more of a subconscious notion than a fully-formed belief, but it's very real. It's the main reason toilet paper made from recycled paper is much less common than toilet paper made without recycled content. If you think about what this kind of phobia against recycled material really represents, it's rather pathetic. Many modern humans are so self-absorbed and arrogant as to believe, deep down, that they are too good to even wipe themselves with recycled material. What does that say about our readiness to make the sacrifices and compromises necessary to achieve sustainability? It's not good.

A Sense of Entitlement

One of the biggest obstacles to sustainability (or to educating people about it) is the fierce sense of entitlement most people seem to have about their unsustainable lifestyles. Whether it's their choice to drive a huge SUV, to illuminate their enormous homes with unnecessary lighting, to take hour-long hot showers or any other obscenely wasteful life choice, people become extremely defensive at the suggestion that such choices are wrong. To such people, wasteful practices are neither right nor wrong. They just perceive them as personal choices that they have some kind of God-given right to make. They refuse to admit or consider that these choices negatively affect others, and as such are beyond what should be allowed under the protections of personal liberty. I have heard many people make the argument that they work hard at their jobs and thus have the right to spend their money as they want, even on items or practices that are clearly unsustainable. Such an attitude misses the point: Just because you can do something doesn't mean you should. That's a simple concept, but one easily obscured by people's belief that they are entitled to any lifestyle they want, regardless of its effects.

Society prohibits lots of activities and practices that are detrimental to the greater good. The fact that some people might want to engage in those practices does not trump the overriding interest in the wellbeing of society as a whole. Hopefully, that perspective will soon extend to unsustainable activities and practices as well. Unsustainable living is not just a personal choice. It hurts everyone, including everyone who has yet to live.

The limits of personal freedom are said to be found where those freedoms begin to infringe on those of another. Everyone has a birthright to a healthy planet, and no one has the right, through their actions, to trample that for wanton personal pleasure.

We have an obligation to each other to take care of this planet as best as we can. As we mature in our understanding of sustainable living, we have an obligation to adopt the best possible practices in our daily lives. No one should defiantly insist they have some kind of God-given right not to. No one is entitled to waste and destroy what others need to survive—what others deserve to enjoy.

Fading to Gray

    A freight train takes longer to start or stop than a car. Lake Superior takes longer to warm up or cool down than a cup of water sitting on the sidewalk. Large systems just change more slowly as a result of their great mass. But with that great mass comes a lot of inertia, and once a change is initiated, it tends to keep building. So it is with the Earth's ecosystems. The biodiversity of this planet is massive indeed, but it's in decline. The movement is so slow, many people don't perceive it, but the momentum of loss has been unleashed and will continue. We are now condemned to endure a long period of loss as biodiversity slowly fades. We are powerless to stop it. Even if we ended all unsustainable practices today, many species are too far down the road to extinction to turn around now. Changes in a system as large as the Earth's ecosystems unfold slowly over decades or centuries. The Earth began losing biodiversity as soon as humans evolved. Everywhere on Earth humans went, accelerated rates of extinction followed. This includes the prehistoric times of our early and middle history as a species. As we spread out of Africa, across Asia and Europe and eventually the Americas, animal species, most often large "mega fauna," disappeared in our wake. And as our civilization continues to grow and become more needy in terms of consumption of natural resources, the Anthropocene is becoming a terrible time for life on Earth. Some of it is bowing out at this point, leaving us increasingly alone on the planetary stage. For those of us who can perceive the loss, it hurts. It's a feeling of loneliness and grief at having been cheated out of enjoying a Garden of Eden. The Earth has so much to give that even after having shed so much, a lot remains, enough to convince many that everything's OK. But these are the same people who wouldn't notice the absence of even the most prominent forms of life.

    Few winter birds are as noticeable as crows and cardinals, the former for the numbers, size and raucous ways, the latter for their bright color. But if they were both to vanish, what percentage of Americans would notice? Many, a sizeable majority I believe, would never even know or care. They would go about life as obliviously as before, and if someone were to inform them that crows and cardinals used to be common but now seem nonexistent, they would feign a moment's interest and then move on, never to think of it again. Given this hopeless ambivalence, how will the plight of coy, retiring species like whip-poor-wills or cerulean warblers ever be known? The sharp decline their numbers have experienced in recent years might as well have been playing out on the dark side of the moon. They and many other species of animals and plants have been severely affected by human land use practices, and most people have no idea whatsoever. For many such species, extinction is probably inevitable.

I once saw an old black-and-white photo of a big game hunter posing with a white rhino he had just shot. When that photo was taken on a blazing hot and sunny day, the colors were bright, the details sharp and the events real, so real as to seem ordinary. Rhinos were plentiful and the deduction of this one from the landscape no doubt seemed inconsequential. So it always is in the present. But add big changes and lots of years, and that seemingly mundane "here and now" becomes an irretrievable past to be mourned and craved with a sad desperation no one would have anticipated back in the day. When I see that old photo today, I wish I could go to that time and place. I wish to see populations of rhinos and countless other species thriving as they did in the 19th century and before. But I can't. All I can do is stare intently through a blurry window into the past and yearn and mourn.

The edges of that old photo seem to fade to a whitish-gray, probably a function of the photographic equipment of that era. As my eyes pan over the picture, they're inevitably drawn to those edges, hungry to see more—more of what was, back then. But those faded edges and blurry background seem to mock my desire for a wider view with more details, more diversity. It's simply not there, and the older that picture gets, the more detail is lost to fading and decay. The corollary to today is obvious. Our planet has been losing biodiversity for a long time. We're on that trajectory now. Actions taken decades ago have put us on that path, and some are only now beginning to make themselves felt. Our decisions to waste and abuse rather than conserve don't always have immediate results. As mentioned above, large systems take longer to react than small ones. The Earth's ecosystems may take decades or centuries to show the full impact of forces absorbed in the past.

A paper published in the September 2010 issue of the journal Bioscience ponders why human well-being seems to be increasing or holding steady while the Earth is increasingly in distress as a result of our actions. In other words, why are we humans not immediately feeling the results of our misuse of the planet's resources? One of four hypotheses the authors propose to explain the paradox is that of "time lags," or the notion that there may be a large lapse between the forces of cause and effect. The authors of that paper concede that they can't muster much scientific proof that time lags explain the paradox. Ironically, the only sure way to prove the time lag effect would be to allow the Earth to decline in a sort of natural experiment resulting in our own demise. The time lag hypothesis certainly seems to be valid of its face. When I look at that old picture, a faded snapshot of a moment in which the Earth was a much richer place, I see a stronger and more vibrant planet, but one that was doomed to become what it is today. Much of the biodiversity lost between then and now faded as a result of actions taken before, not after, the photo was taken. And so it is that much of what we have done over the last several decades will continue to revisit us in spades long into the future. I can sense the slow but deliberate decline of the Earth's richness. I see it in negative when I juxtapose that old picture with the reality of today and am struck with what is different, what is lost.

Not Our Good Side

Bacteria put into a Petri dish filled with a nutritious medium will multiply and flourish. Their population will grow to whatever level the available resources will permit. Once the finite medium in which they had been growing is depleted, their numbers will decline, eventually to zero. They will never, not once, ponder their condition. They will never assess their surroundings or the resources they are utilizing. They will just live until they die. Unfortunately, few humans are any more discerning than bacteria when it comes to a real awareness of their surroundings or resources. I recently heard someone tell a friend that his television looked like it had seen better days and might need replacing soon. His response struck me as one of the most offensive things I'd heard in quite some time: "Those things don't last as long as they used to, but they're so cheap at Wal-Mart, I just run 'em 'til the blow up and then throw 'em out with the garbage." I felt like telling him that the TVs he had been mindlessly tossing into the landfill contain and depend upon a variety of rare Earth elements experts say will be depleted soon if we keep using them at current rates. The least he could do is return the old TV's for recycling. I wondered if he ever thought about how our current lifestyle, which is replete with devices like his flat-screen color TV, can possibly be maintained very long into the future, given the resources it takes to make it all happen. Without even asking, I knew that he hadn't. He hadn't thought about that or any other aspect of his lifestyle of consumption. He bought, used and replaced TVs because they were there. That's all. Except for the price tag expressed in dollars, there was no awareness of what it cost, in resources, to put that TV on his living room table. The same can be said of cell phones, microwave ovens, laundry detergent with "stain lifters" and anything else you can think of that is a part of our modern lives but that cannot be found anywhere in nature. People use these things with absolutely no thought as to whether they are sustainable, no thought as to whether their creation, use and disposal is an intolerable burden on the Earth's systems, no thought as to whether they are necessary, no thought as to whether an alternative is available, no thought as to whether it's a good idea. Like the bacteria, there is no thought at all. We just accept what is around us and use it with no consideration whatsoever.

In many ways, this blind acceptance and use, without question, of what we find within our grasp can look like a lack of intelligence. It's a very unflattering angle from which to observe human intellect. But we are the same beings who are intelligent enough to engineer and manufacture all these unsustainable items and practices, so it cannot be that we are utterly stupid. I guess the best you can say is that the way humans are burning through millions of years of accumulated resources to subsidize a few hundred years of extravagance exposes a facet of our being that is definitely not our good side.

Campsite Blues

Have you ever gone camping or perhaps hunting with one or more people in a remote area that required the establishment of a base camp? If so, you selected a campsite in a location that bore no trace of human presence, probably a flat area for the tent with a prevailing wind to take the smoke from the camp fire away from, not into, your face. Having a water source and plenty of firewood nearby also may have influenced your choice. The first night spent in such a place is always special, almost magical. It's the location that gives it that magic. You selected this wonderful place and can take pride in having done so. It's as if everything good about it is owing to your judgment, prudence and vision. Even the moon and stars in the sky overhead seem to offer testament to your skill in selecting just the right place to build this wonderful respite, this welcoming, albeit temporary, homestead for you and your companions.

Living, if only for a few days, in a completely unspoiled area is exciting, a pleasure like no other. But for me, that excitement can deflate as quickly as a bursting balloon if too much human activity mars the unspoiled quality of the place. Paths develop quickly around the campsite from forays to gather firewood and tend to other necessities. Telltale signs of human activity—an empty soup can waiting to be packed out, an errant crust of bread, or a loose string from a bedroll can be all it takes to make that wild place seem domestic. Even the campfire itself—the focal point of the site—can lose its magic when it begins to look more like an old, overused pit than a pyre of fresh embers on virgin ground. And when a previously magical campsite begins to feel old, it's the most disappointing brand of mundane there is. It's the campsite blues. This feeling usually strikes me in the morning. Maybe morning reveals the signs of use more starkly. Maybe I'm more susceptible then. Whatever the cause, the feeling makes me want to pack up camp and move on. It can make that previously unspoiled campsite feel like a Spartan version of civilization. Gone is the freshness, the newness. It's like being home again, but without the amenities or conveniences. What's the point?

It's pretty much impossible to prevent the campsite blues. Eventually, just the utter familiarity of a heavily used campsite will strip it of its initial magic. Perhaps because much of our existence as a species was spent nomadically, we are hardwired to want to move on and look for new, untouched wild places to call home. How do the current land use practices we employ in residential, commercial and industrial areas fit with the instinct some of us feel to value untouched, unspoiled places? Much of the United States is increasingly without wild places. Our footprint has expanded to the point that it's impossible to escape it in many areas. You don't have to go

Embracing Sustainability

camping to get the campsite blues. The feeling can sneak up on you any time it seems that you just can't get away from that human footprint. To know that feeling is to know one more reason why it's important to leave as much of the Earth in as pristine, unaltered a condition as possible.

What Are You Going to Do With It?

I've always felt that buying land is one of the best purchases anyone could make. To me, land that remains unspoiled by human "development" is more valuable than any other material investment one could make. I see an intrinsic value in nature, and thus in the land that supports it. I bought my first piece of land, a 249-acre diamond in the rough of rural West Virginia, when I was 28. It was the culmination of years of yearning for a piece of land I could call my own—a place I didn't need someone else's permission to go upon. I soon found out that holding the deed for a piece of land doesn't change much. "Ownership" of land is a very temporary state. One human lifetime is a very short-term lease on an item that will be around for millions of years. The ownership and fate of a piece of land is subject to a chain of custody stretching over the eons. Few things bring one's own mortality into as clear a focus as understanding how insignificant we are—how puny a stake our deed of trust gives us in the legacy of a piece of land. We claim to possess it. We are the legal owners of record. But countless entities have had just as much right to it in the past, whether they were humans before us or wildlife who defended it as their territory. And countless more will inherit it during a future in which our tenure will be wholly forgotten. I enjoy and appreciate land equally, whether I own it or not. That said, ownership of land does bring a certain comfort. It's accompanied, however, with the realization that we're neither the first nor the last to call this place their own.

When new friends or acquaintances find out I own acreage, many invariably ask, "What are you going to do with it?" I've heard that question many dozens of times from as many people, and it has always bothered me. I've never known quite how to respond. I used to assume the reason for wanting to own a piece of land would be patently obvious and clear, but it's not. Many people cannot fathom why someone would want to buy land unless they had some tangible use in mind for it. That there would be satisfaction just in ownership is incomprehensible to them. This inability to understand the allure of land ownership stems from a general lack of respect or appreciation for land. For years, I struggled to answer the insolent "What are you going to do with it?" question. If I had just bought a saw, I could say, "I'm going to cut wood with it." If I had just bought a pen, I could say, "I'm going to write with it." If I had just bought a gun, I could say, "I'm going to shoot it." Those responses would all be understood. But if I were to respond to the land question with, "I'm not going to do anything with it. I'm going to go out onto it and marvel at its glories, both small and large. I'm going to watch it work as it dances in wondrous harmony with the changing seasons. I'm going to notice which plants and animals find it suitable for their needs, and I'm then going to give thanks for their presence," I suspect my reply would be met with either a double blink or a blank stare. What I would like to say is this: "What you mean to ask is, do I intend to extract its natural resources in a way that would diminish the richness of the land and the diversity of life on it? Do I intend to build or place unnatural objects or manipulate its surface, displacing what would naturally be there? Do I intend to do damage that will remain long after I'm gone? Do I have any unsustainable land use plans? No, I do not. I intend simply to protect the fertility and biodiversity of this place. I plan to participate in the play of life now showing on its stage. I hope to leave it stronger and richer than it was when I found it. And I will stand in reverence and awe of all that it is." That would be my answer. That's what I'm going to do with it.

On Our Best Behavior

The biggest obstacle to achieving sustainability on a societal scale is people's unwillingness to forgo individual convenience for the sake of the greater good. We don't want to give up our current lifestyle, even as it becomes increasingly obvious that it's untenable. However, there is plenty of precedent for people collectively embracing regulation of individual behavior for the greater good. The rule of law and our willingness to obey everything from stop lights to restrictions against murder show that we can agree to live in a way that makes the world better for all of us. Particularly for serious crimes of violence or theft, we don't comply with the law simply to avoid jail time. Our good behavior is the result of convictions we have about right and wrong. Most of us don't feel repressed by the fact we're not allowed to rob banks or mug our neighbors. We feel better about ourselves when we live civil lives. We take pride in being the kind of people who choose to do what's right because we want to, not because we have to.

The disconnect that's preventing this kind of willingness to live right from ushering in a new era of sustainability is that there's no history to support it. Crime and other anti-social behavior were proved maladaptive long ago. Even ancient cultures saw the wisdom in eschewing them. And although the Mayan and Roman empires probably fell because they were unsustainable, there's no universally understood cultural taboo against unsustainable living. Coupled with this is the fact that sustainability has been highly politicized. The fact that sustainability has become so polarizing means people whose belief systems put them at odds with sustainability find it easy to rationalize their position.

Cultural norms and values vary from society to society. Americans are prudish by European standards when it comes to nudity. Middle Eastern countries are even more so. Asian cultures have traditionally placed a great emphasis on excelling in school and work settings. The point is, societies are not the same the world over. Differences can and do arise. The conservation ethic has been rising in several parts of the world for a while now. Europe, Australia and America have all seen increases in "green" initiatives, but the politicization of the green concept has made it impossible for it to be universally embraced the way non-politicized cultural norms have been. As long as sustainability is one of those concepts that breaks down along conservative/liberal lines, it will not achieve widespread acceptance. If the rancor and controversy can be neutralized, acceptance as a cultural norm will be possible. Most likely, change like that will require two or more generations. The problems arising from unsustainable living may speed the process somewhat, but right now, we have the option of turning our backs on sustainability. If someone is a known murderer or rapist, people will stigmatize him. But nobody will think a person is horrible or impugn his character for not embracing sustainability. A significant number of people take that pass, either knowingly or unknowingly.

As a society, we are quick to jump on any bandwagon that grants us easy living or instant gratification. Sustainable practices seldom offer those attributes. The idea of economic growth is a prime example. It has pervaded popular culture, politics, business and our personal psyches. Everyone and every institution seems to have embraced the notion that growth is necessary and good for the well-being of our society and our economy. Evidence to the contrary is plentiful and in plain sight. The reasons why perpetual growth is impossible are all around us, and it doesn't take a genius to understand them. Society should have connected the dots by now, but we want to be blind. We want to continue the ride we're on for as long as we can. And since it's not taboo to act as if economic growth can continue forever, most people are all too happy to do so. Until social pressures demand otherwise, our behavior will not change, and the universal implementation of sustainability will remain elusive. But when it does, our desire to be good people will command a sustainability imperative. Our best behavior will include sustainable behavior.

The Importance, Complexity and Fragility of Soil

One inch of topsoil takes about 750 years to form. Rocks, minerals and organic matter weather and erode to produce sand, silt and clay, which are the three components of all soil types. Lichens (algae and fungus in a symbiotic relationship) contribute acid, which speeds the process and enables certain chemical reactions. Bacteria, fungi and micro-organisms (notably actinomycetes) exist in unimaginable numbers in every ounce of soil. But they don't just exist in the soil. They are the soil. Without them, it would not function. They partner with each other and with plant roots to create nutrients and add nitrogen that plants need to grow.

Green plants are the foundation of all terrestrial food chains on the planet. These plants, on which all life depends, take carbon, hydrogen and oxygen from the air and water to create organic mass. But 15 other elements must be present in various combinations and concentrations to support rich and diverse plant life: N, P, K, Ca, Mg, S, B, Cu, Cl, Fe, Mn, Mo, Zn, Ni, and Cobalt come from deeper subsoils and rock layers and are only available because of the highly choreographed relationships between the bacteria, fungi, microorganisms and roots that serve as the lifeblood of dirt. Take them away or upset their balance and the fertility and productivity of the soil will be lost. It takes a very long time for these elements to accumulate adequately in the topsoil to support high quality plant and tree life. Over eons, the soil organizes itself into layers—each one home to a unique host of bacteria, fungi and microorganisms. If these layers are disturbed, they can take almost as long to re-organize as they did to form—that is to say millennia. If they are removed altogether and replaced with rocky overburden, soil will not exist in the area for eons. Most plants and trees need special bacterial and fungal partners to work with their roots. Without them, they will not grow well or at all. An apt analogy is the bacteria in our own gut. Without them, we would perish.

There are hundreds of thousands of different species of bacteria in a single spoonful of healthy soil. Talk about biodiversity! That's a mix of life more complex than anything we can see or even imagine, but it exists in the dirt right beneath our feet, or at least it's supposed to. This countless throng of microbe species has evolved into an equally varied number of micro-ecosystems. They must be present in just the right amounts and proportions in order for the soil to support the plant life we currently see utilizing it. Change the mix on a microscopic level and the equation changes all the way up the food chain.

The thousands of species of fungi present in the same spoonful of dirt also must be present in the right amount and proportions for the soil to continue to function as it currently does. The relationships are fascinating.

Embracing Sustainability

For instance, the fungi are locked in a kind of dance with the bacteria in which they (the fungi) secrete antibiotics that keep the bacteria in check and regulate the whole interaction. When the complexity of soil is understood, it's not an exaggeration to say that the soil is itself a giant organism. According to James Nardi of the University of Chicago, there is so much life in properly functioning dirt that just the top six inches of topsoil on an acre of land contains microorganisms with a metabolic capacity equal to 50,000 human beings. That's a powerful life force, but if the soil is disturbed (something most human land use practices result in), much of that life force is snuffed out. To re-ignite it will require time on a scale we're not used to contemplating. By our standards, the loss is permanent.

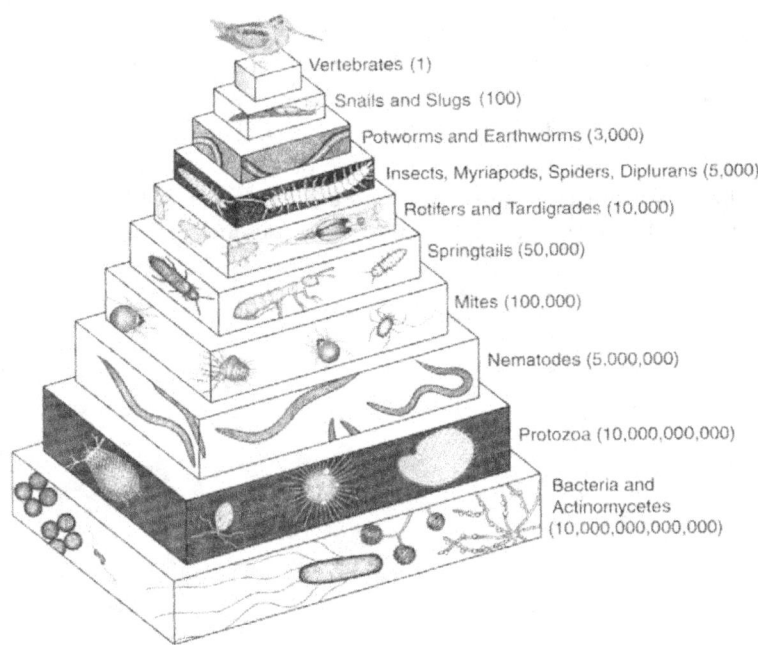

Figure 1. A foodweb pyramid showing the number of organism present in one square meter of properly functioning soil. Reproduced with permission of James Nardi.

Aldo Leopold wrote of the difference between the north and south slopes of Spessart Mountain in Germany. For centuries, the south slope has grown tremendous oak forests, while the north slope, which should have better forests because it would be moister, supports only scotch pine. The explanation for the mystery took scientists a long time to figure out. No surprise, it stems from land use practices hundreds of years ago. Clearcutting and grazing of livestock on the north side several centuries ago altered the mix of microorganisms in the soil. Despite attempts to put things right, the land is unable to do what it once did and will remain so diminished for many more generations. The profound impact on Spessart Mountain was the result of merely changing the surface use. No movement or mixing of soil layers occurred. The damage the occurs when earth-moving equipment reconfigures the land is much longer lasting than what happened on Spessart Mountain about 300 years ago. The damage our roads, cities and industries have caused to the soil will not be forgotten until the Earth enters another epoch of geologic time. It is tragic on both a practical and a philosophical level. I don't think many people realize the harm being done. The saying "cheaper than dirt" shows the low level of respect or appreciation people have for the skin that covers our planet and supports the life found here. People think dirt is nothing but dark colored, inert material that has little value. To most, it is merely something to be trampled upon, and in their minds, it exists in inexhaustible quantities and cannot be harmed. But the damage we have done to soil since the industrial revolution is vast. The decrease in productivity of the soil resulting from human land use practices is among the worst affronts we have committed against this planet. The effects will be among the longest lasting of the detrimental legacies we leave behind.

All That's Lost

The purpose of this chapter is to show, in the most visible way possible, what is lost when we humans engage in unsustainable practices. Mountaintop removal coal mining is perhaps the best (or worst) land use practice to analyze for this purpose. Millions of acres of precious forest and thousands of miles of pristine streams have been obliterated by it. The energy produced is something much of America has partaken of, which means most of us are complicit. Although MTR operations are massive, they are hard to see because they're perpetrated in the mountains of Appalachia, a place many Americans don't even know exists. It makes the region an easy target, as well as an easy victim to ignore. The unfortunate irony of it is that Appalachia is rich in coal and also rich in wildlife, or at least it is until the coal companies strip the tops off its mountains and dump the debris into the valleys between them, burying the streams found there.

The scope of what's lost in a MTR site is inestimable. There's no comparison between the biodiversity found on an acre of Appalachian forestland and that found on an acre of land in Wyoming, another of the country's top coal-producing regions. When people hear the term MTR, many imagine mining on rocky, snow-packed peaks above the tree line with relatively little life clinging to them. The mountains destroyed by MTR are nothing like that at all. They are rich and verdant from top to bottom, resplendent oases teaming with elegant plants and animals, some of which are found nowhere else. If this sounds like a tropical rainforest in South America, you're not far off in terms of the diversity of species harbored or in the irrevocable loss that occurs when industry sets up shop in this evolutionary wonderland—this ecological Garden of Eden.

Here are some before-and-after pictures that demonstrate all that's lost in this practice:

Stream Before

Stream After

Embracing Sustainability

Woods Before

Embracing Sustainability

Woods After

Embracing Sustainability

Forest Floor Before

Forest Floor After

Mountains Before

Mountains After

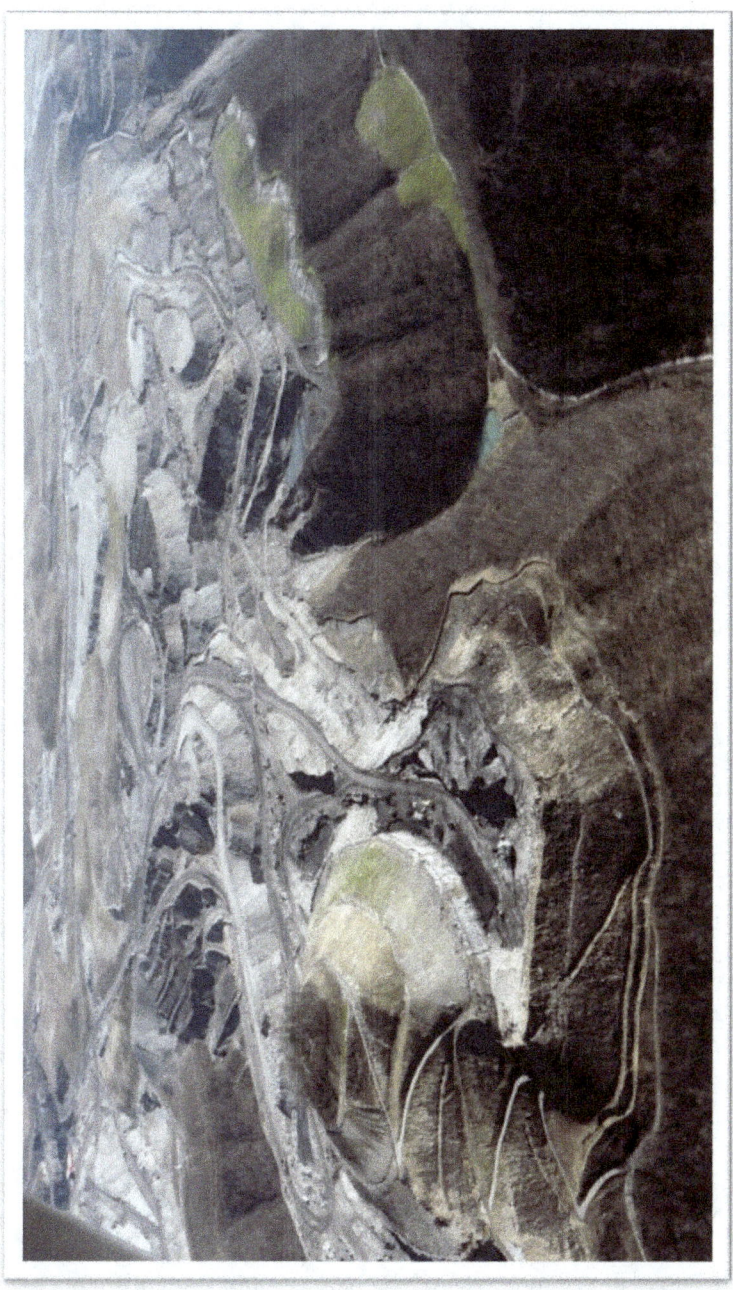

So what is lost? Table 1 lists species that are killed in the stripping process. These are species unable to outrun the bulldozers, draglines and dynamite charges that rip through the area. These are species that suffer 100 percent mortality rates from the mining process. Thousands upon thousands of individuals are crushed, ripped apart or buried alive (or half alive) as the Earth is raped. Along the edges of the destruction, others are maimed only to crawl off and suffer lingering deaths. To these species, the coal operations are like the shock and awe of a war zone. Our assault rips their world apart and violates the sanctity of their bodies in the most violent ways. Skin and surface parts are driven into the depths of their cores while bones and parts that should never see the light of day are brought to the outside. Internal organs are squeezed out of every orifice of the body, sometimes while the animal is still alive, trying in vain to crawl to safety, its escape slowed by the dragging trail of entrails. The eyes of these animals always look surprisingly large when they have erupted completely out of their sockets and dangle from stalks of muscle and optic nerves still attached to their crushed skulls. In death, many will temporarily retain some of their beautiful colors and markings, even when covered in blood or the grey-brown slurry created when a combination of body fluids are comingled with dirt to form a mud that cakes the corpse as if in a final insult. If this description sounds radical and offensive, it's because what happens during the mining process is radical and offensive. To downplay the situation by merely saying that many animals are killed would be to cheat the truth of its right to be known. Take a close look at the list of animals in Table 1. Now imagine taking a sledge hammer and smashing the life out of each and every one. Then do it again, and again—thousands of times. What kind of a person could stomach such carnage? Who could condone that atrocity as an acceptable way to power our lights and televisions and iPods? If you've ever thought of the coal industry as a normal and routine fixture of our society, the answer to the preceding question is, unfortunately, you.

The animals in Table 1, all of which are endemic to the region, will be killed if they are present on the site when stripping commences. Most cannot flee the area. Many will react by hiding underground, which ensures they will be buried alive. Others are simply not fast enough to get away in time. In the case of animals that sleep the winter away such as black bears, strictly nocturnal animals such as bats, or insects during vulnerable stages of their life cycle, stripping when they are inactive will likely result in them being killed. Obviously, all vegetation in the area is destroyed by the mining. Some plants, such as ginseng and goldenseal, are protected by regulations. Digging them out of season or in excess of the harvest quota is punishable by law, but coal operations can destroy all they want with impunity. The same is true of

Embracing Sustainability

protected species of non-game animals. It is illegal to kill most of these animals. Some require permits to even collect as live specimens, but again, the coal industry can kill them en masse and no one dares to suggest that it's a problem.

Table 1. Animals Killed During Stripping

Banded darter	Rainbow darter	Headwater darter
Orangethroat darter	Johnny darter	Greenside darter
Cumberland plateau darter	Aarow darter	Fantail darter
Dusky darter	Teardrop darter	Logperch
Rosyside dace	Southern redbelly dace	Blacknose dace
Longnose dace	Creek chub	Central stoneroller
Scarlet shiner	Popeye shiner	Telescope shiner
Mimic shiner	Silverjaw minnow	Fathead minnow
Bluntnose minnow	White sucker	Northern hog sucker
Brindled madtom	Mottled sculpin	Big sandy crayfish
Eastern box turtle	Midland painted turtle	Jefferson salamander
Spotted salamander	Marbled salamander	Red spotted newt
Northern dusky salamander	Mountain dusky salamander	Appalachian seal salamander
Blackbelly salamander	Red back salamander	Ravine salamander
Slimy salamander	Cumberland plateau salamander	Wehrle's salamander
Four-toed salamander	Northern spring salamander	Kentucky spring salamander
Midland mud salamander	Northern red salamander	Green salamander
Northern two-lined salamander	Longtail salamander	Eastern spadefoot
Eastern American toad	Fowler's toad	Northern spring peeper
Gray treefrog	Mountain chorus frog	Green frog
Wood frog	Northern leopard frog	Ground skink
Five-lined skink	Broadhead skink	Northern coal skink
Queen snake	Northern brown snake	Northern redbelly snake
Eastern ribbon snake	Eastern garter snake	Eastern earth snake
Eastern hognose snake	Northern ringneck snake	Eastern worm snake
Northern black racer	Rough green snake	Eastern smooth green snake
Black rat snake	Black kingsnake	Eastern milk snake
Northern copperhead	Timber rattlesnake	Eastern chipmunk
Eastern spotted skunk	Striped skunk	Virginia opossum
Allegheny woodrat	Groundhog	American deer mouse
White footed mouse	Golden mouse	Woodland vole
Woodland jumping mouse	Smoky shrew	Rock shrew
Pygmy shrew	Least shrew	Northern short-tailed shrew
Hairy-tailed mole	Eastern small-footed myotis	Little brown bat
Indiana bat	Gray bat	Northern myotis
Silverhaired bat	Eastern pipistrelle	Big brown bat
Eastern red bat	Hoary bat	Rafinesque's big-eared bat
American mink	Long-tailed weasel	Least weasel

The loss doesn't end with the merciless and brutal destruction of the life shown in table 1. There are animals, mostly birds, that can flee the mining area, but for the most part, neither they nor any of their kind will ever return to the areas because they require, as habitat, the forests that existed before mining. Those forests will never again grow on the mined sites because the very specific soil types they need have been permanently lost. Table 2 lists some of the animal species that will never again live on MTR sites. They are

Embracing Sustainability

extirpated from these areas, and their return will need to be measured not in decades or centuries, but in geologic time. Their absence for so long means that the MTR sites will contribute nothing in terms of future reproduction to populations of these species. Over time, the cumulative loss of recruitment will be staggering. It is not practical in a work of this length to include all the plant and insect species that will also be extirpated from these sites. Just including affected moths more than doubled the length of table 2. It's not that plants and insects are less important, only that there are so many species of each as to make listing them unrealistic. Their great numbers add significantly to the toll mountaintop removal mining takes on the biodiversity of Appalachia.

Table 2. Animals Unable to Reestablish Breeding Populations

Southern flying squirrel	Yellow-billed cuckoo	Hooded warbler
Eastern fox squirrel	Black-billed cuckoo	Canada warbler
Eastern gray squirrel	Great-horned owl	American redstart
Golden mouse	Eastern screech owl	Northern oriole
Woodland vole	Barred owl	Scarlet tanager
Woodland jumping mouse	Whip-poor-will	Summer tanager
Smoky shrew	Pileated woodpecker	Northern cardinal
Rock shrew	Red-bellied woodpecker	Rose-breasted grosbeak
Indiana bat	Red-headed woodpecker	Purple finch
Little brown bat	Downy woodpecker	Eastern towee
Eastern small-footed bat	Hairy woodpecker	Banded darter
Gray bat	Yellow-bellied sapsucker	Rainbow darter
Northern myotis	Great-crested flycatcher	Headwater darter
Silver-haired bat	Eastern phoebe	Orangethroat darter
Eastern pipistrelle	Acadian flycatcher	Johnny darter
Big brown bat	Least flycatcher	Greenside darter
Eastern red bat	Eastern wood pewee	Cumberland plateau darter
Hoary bat	Blue jay	Arrow darter
Rafinesque's big-eared bat	American crow	Fantail darter
Black bear	Black-capped chickadee	Dusky darter
Jefferson salamander	Tufted titmouse	Teardrop darter
Spotted salamander	White-breasted nuthatch	Logperch
Marbled salamander	Brown creeper	Rosyside dace
Red-spotted newt (red eft)	Wood thrush	Southern redbelly dace
Northern dusky salamander	Hermit thrush	Blacknose dace
Mountain dusky salamander	Swainson's thrush	Longnose dace
Appalachian seal salamander	Veery	Scarlet shiner
Blackbelly salamander	White-throated sparrow	Popeye shiner
Red back salamander	Ruby-crowned kinglet	Telescope shiner
Ravine salamander	Golden-crowned kinglet	Mimic shiner
Slimy salamander	Blue-grey gnatcatcher	Fathead minnow
Cumberland plateau salamander	Cedar waxwing	Bluntnose minnow
Wehrle's salamander	Solitary vireo	Silverjaw minnow
Four-toed salamander	White-eyed vireo	Central stoneroller
Northern spring salamander	Red-eyed vireo	Creek chub
Kentucky salamander	Worm-eating warbler	White sucker
Midland mud salamander	Black-and-white warbler	Northern hog sucker
Northern red salamander	Blue-winged warbler	Mottled sculpin
Green salamander	Northern parula	Brindled madtom

Embracing Sustainability

Northern two-lined salamander
Cooper's hawk
Sharp-shinned hawk
Red-tailed hawk
Red-shouldered hawk
American kestrel
Rough-legged hawk
Broad-winged hawk
Ruffed grouse
Locust underwing (moth)
Promethea moth
Rosy maple moth
Northern eudeilinia
Eubaphe mendica
White fringed emerald
Signate melanolophia
Linden looper
Least-marked euchlaena
Maple spanworm
Lemon plagodis
Fervid plagodis
Oak besma
Curve-toothed geometer
Spotted apatelodes
Pink-striped oakworm moth
Ash sphinx
Waved sphinx
Twin-spotted sphinx
Georgina prominent
Elegant prominent
Drexel's datana
White-dotted prominent
Mottled prominent
White-blotched heterocampa
Unicorn prominent
Red-humped oakworm
Yellow-based tussock moth
White-marked tussock moth
Reverse haploa
Grayish fan foot
Dimorphic snout
Deceptive snout
Small necklace
Black-patched graylet
Epione underwing
Angus' underwing
Residua underwing
Tearful underwing
Youthful underwing
Ilia underwing
Clinton's underwing
Connubial underwing
Common oak moth
False underwing
Intent zale
Brown panapoda
Eyed baileya
Close-banded yellowhorn

Black-throated green warbler
Black-throated blue warbler
Cerulean warbler
Yellow-throated warbler
Blackburnian warbler
Ovenbird
Kentucky warbler
Prothonotary warbler
Imperial moth
Sweetheart underwing (moth)
Polyphemus moth
Luna moth
Rosy hooktip
Three spotted fillip
Common angle
Small phigalia
Gray spring moth
Oak beauty
Elm spanworm
Purple plagodis
Hollow spotted plagodis
Hemlock looper
Scalloped sack-bearer
Spiny oakworm moth
Eastern buck moth
Pawpaw sphinx
Catalpa sphinx
Small-eyed sphinx
Double-toothed prominent
White furcular
Contracted datana
Linden prominent
Oblique heterocampa
Variable oak-leaf caterpillar
Black-blotched schizura
Orange-humped oakworm
Streaked tussock moth
Scarlet-winged lichen moth
Hickory tussock moth
Morbid owlet
Mottled snout
Gray-edged snout
Dotted graylet
Thin-lined owlet
Habilis underwing
Judith's underwing
Yellow-gray underwing
Oldwife underwing
Sad underwing
Yellow-banded underwing
Similar underwing
Girlfriend underwing
Figure seven moth
Maple zale
Horrid zale
Curve-lined owlet
Sleeping baileya
The laugher

Gray treefrog
Northern spring peeper
Wood frog
Grape leaf skeletonizer (moth)
Wild cherry sphinx (moth)
Hebrew (moth)
Spotted tiger moth
White-marked tussock moth
Virginia creeper sphinx (moth)
Tulip tree beauty (moth)
Regal moth
Dogwood thyatirid
Shiny gray carpet
Red-fringed emerald
Bent-line gray
Spiny cankerworm
Common lytrosis
Pale beauty
Kent's geometer
Straight-lined plagodis
Straw besma
Curved-lined looper
Melsheimer's sack-bearer
Orange-tipped oakworm moth
Tulip tree silkmoth
Elm sphinx
Laurel sphinx
Walnut sphinx
Black-rimmed prominent
Angus' datana
Walnut caterpillar moth
Angulose prominent
Small heterocampa
Double-lined prominent
White-headed prominent
Gray-patched prominent
Definite tussock moth
Fall webworm
Lettered fan foot
Baltimore snout
White-lined snout
Red-footed snout
White-lined graylet
The penitent
Robinson's underwing
Obscure underwing
Widow underwing
Clouded underwing
The bride
Scarlet underwing
The little nymph
Little-lined underwing
Maple looper
Colorful zale
Red-lined panapoda
Three-spotted nola
Saddled yellowhorn
Ruddy dagger

Embracing Sustainability

American dagger	Funerary dagger	Delightful dagger
Pleasant dagger	speared dagger	Nondescript dagger
Interrupted dagger	Great oak dagger	Ovate dagger
Medium dagger	Hesitant dagger	Small oak dagger
Retarded dagger	Afflicted dagger	Yellow-haired dagger
Night-wandering dagger	Long-winged dagger	Streaked dagger
Green marvel	Figure eight sallow	Roland's sallow
Chosen sallow	Fawn sallow	Grote's sallow
Broad-lined sallow	Fringe-tree sallow	Turbulent phosphila
Spotted phosphila	The slowpoke	Ash-tip borer
Sensitive fern borer	Dimorphic pinion	Hemina pinion
Grote's pinion	Dowdy pinion	Mustard sallow
Straight-toothed sallow	Morrison's sallow	Sloping sallow
Silky sallow	American dun-bar	Ruby quaker
Garman's quaker	Gray quaker	Norman's quaker
Intractable quaker	Distinct quaker	Bicolored woodgrain
Confused woodgrain	Fluid arches	Northern scurfy quaker
Sheathed quaker		

A 1,000-acre MTR site will take years to mine, and will leave a permanent dead zone on the Earth the size of a city, but in total, that 1,000-acre sacrifice will provide enough electricity to meet the nation's residential electrical usage for only about two days. That means that if we wanted to power just our homes (not businesses or factories) with MTR coal, we would need to strip mine an area the size of New Jersey every 30 years. Think about that, and remember that for each acre lost, one of the costs of this power will be an immediate death sentence for the animals shown in Table 1 and the future absence of the animals shown in Table 2. These heavy tolls are among the saddest externalities imaginable. They are also completely unnecessary, completely avoidable. We don't need the coal from MTR mines. Reducing our energy usage through conservation and efficiency would allow us to successfully meet our needs through renewables, primarily solar. I've been doing so myself since 2011, and many other people do too. But states like West Virginia have sold their souls to the coal industry, and will allow it to do whatever it wants—no matter what the cost and despite all that's lost.

Figure 2.   **The Cost of Coal Comes in Every Color**

The illustration on the following page shows just a handful of the species lost through MTR coal mining, either at the time of mining or in the future because of habitat loss. The loss of this biodiversity is but a fraction of the total cost of mountaintop removal, but it shows that the cost of coal comes in every color.

Too Big to Handle, But Not Too Big to Fail

Human society is like an inexperienced logger felling a big tree. We have the tools it takes to move something much bigger than ourselves, but not the skills or know-how to do so in a safe and controlled way. We humans are definitely capable of impacting the Earth's natural systems, but we lack the competence necessary to know what result our actions will bring. So like the amateur lumberjack, it's not long before very powerful forces start moving in the wrong directions, with disastrous effects.

Yesterday, I heard a news report that monarch butterfly populations made a slight rebound this year, but their population is still down precipitously from over a billion 25 years ago to about 30 million today. The experts aren't sure exactly why, but they believe a variety of factors convened to decimate monarch populations. Pesticides, mainly Roundup, that kill milkweed (critically necessary as a food source) are thought to be the primary culprit.

Today, I just finished reading an article in Northern Woodlands magazine about the serious decline in moose numbers across the northern United States, from Wyoming and Minnesota across New England. Moose numbers are down to less than half of what they were 20 years ago. Again, it's a tapestry of causes no one saw coming that seem to be responsible. An increase in the number of winter ticks, a significant moose parasite that seems to be flourishing as winters become milder, is getting part of the blame. Also, a type of parasitic brainworm carried by but harmless to whitetail deer is fatal when it spreads to moose. And so as whitetail populations expand into moose range, partly thanks to climate change, moose are confronting a threat they have never faced before.

The pattern of mysterious declines such as those seen in monarch butterflies and moose is starting to sound familiar. Monarchs and moose are just two of a growing cadre of animals in decline. The startling similarity for most of them is that no one predicted their decline, and even after it was noticed, the causes were hard to identify. The inescapable conclusion to be taken from this is that our unsustainable lifestyle is touching off all sorts of ecological malfunctions that we can neither predict nor stop. The systems that govern life on Earth are beyond our comprehension and control. And while they are too big for us to handle, they are, unfortunately, not too big for us to destroy. They are not too big to fail.

For Better or Worse—Determinism, Free Will and Social Change

Is it even possible for society to achieve sustainability? This book proceeds on the premise that it must if we are to continue to exist. This book also discusses plenty of pathways and processes through which sustainability could be achieved, at least theoretically. But being theoretically possible doesn't mean that something is realistically possible. Life is full of utopian yearnings for which there is a hopeless disconnect between the two. Social scientific theories of determinism argue back and forth about whether we have free will to affect our destiny or whether we are powerless to create the future of our exact choosing. Clearly, we have some degree of free will and can consciously affect the outcomes of some things. Both in our individual lives and as a society, even as a species, we can and do make choices. But there's plenty of evidence that we cannot do so at all times, in all places and for all matters. For example, it was inevitable that someone, somewhere would unlock the genie of nuclear energy. Given our thirst for scientific exploration and invention, there would have been no way to will that discovery from happening. And now that we know how to split atoms, there is no way to will that Pandora's box out of existence. Would the world be a better place without nuclear weapons? Any reasonable person who lived through the Cold War would say "Yes." Would it be possible to get every nation and faction on Earth to agree to give up nukes if they have them and to never pursue them if they don't? The answer to that question is an equally certain "No." Even though we would all be better off if nuclear annihilation were not possible, it seems as though we could never bring ourselves to lift that dark threat hanging over our heads, even though we theoretically could if we would all agree to just do so.

The question is, is achieving sustainability also something we should all want to do, but, despite free will, cannot bring ourselves to do? I don't know. Time will tell, and finding the answer may perhaps be the greatest test of our human ingenuity and adaptability ever proffered. If we pass that test, if we cross the divide that separates sustainable from unsustainable, we would emerge as a changed species—different in a way more profound than seen during all but a few epic transitions in our history such as the Stone Age, the development of language and the agricultural revolution. Envisioning ourselves in that future, envisioning the kind of beings who could bring themselves to that lofty achievement, offers a glimpse of a culture fundamentally different from the one we now know. If we someday fully embrace sustainability with all its trappings, we will have changed from individuals and a culture that looks for immediate solutions and instant gratification to beings whose vision and plans and activities are built around the long view. We would consider only those lifestyles and societal practices that held the promise of true sustainability. Anything less would be perceived as foolish and imprudent and would never receive our individual or collective acceptance.

I believe humans will ultimately come to embrace sustainability, but not before suffering a devastating population crash and political/economic/social collapse. The sting of that major resetting event will, I hope, be a lesson we never forget. Each step of our evolution as a species has accelerated our growth and increased the unsustainability of our existence. In 200,000 years, we have yet to come up against the hard, unyielding limits of sustainability. Given our trajectory, it is inevitable that we will, and fairly soon. That tribulation will be a first in human history, and human history from that point on will be fundamentally different. The lesson of sustainability will have been learned the hard way. Hopefully, it will not just be the low point in a cycle we are doomed to repeat. Hopefully, the lessons learned and wisdom gained will carry forward through future generations. Perhaps historians in the future will classify human history into periods of "pre-sustainability" and "post sustainability." If so, the latter will eventually become the longer of the two periods, and although the advancement of human society will progress more slowly in the post sustainability period than the flash-in-a-pan "development" we've known until now, our post sustainability era will eventually be where the greatest of human accomplishments occur.

We are currently causing the sixth mass extinction in our planet's history. If we survive it and enter that post-sustainability period, we may last long enough as a species to be here when the cause of the seventh mass extinction presents itself. If we have spent the intervening time building our scientific knowledge base and technological capabilities, it is just possible that we will be in a position to intervene and lessen or stop that extinction event altogether. What a day that would be! What redemption! What atonement for our past sins! The day when human impact on the Earth goes into the black and tips into the "more good than harm" range is the day when we can truly claim the title of "stewards" of this planet. Will we make it? Can we make it? Time will reveal our future, be it for better or worse.

Saving What?

"Save the Earth" is a cliché everyone has heard, but what does it really mean? Clearly, that phrase has been widely circulated in our society, but ironically, few people, even those who have invoked it, know what it means. Theoretically, it could have two distinct meanings. In the first, "save" could mean to conserve the Earth, to not squander or exhaust our planet. This interpretation would belie a desire to make sure that enough of the Earth (and its resources) remain for the future. This notion resonates with the theme of sustainability.

The second meaning of "save the Earth" would use "save" to mean protect or defend against a destructive force. Clearly, there are destructive forces that do grievous harm to the Earth. One need look no farther than a mountaintop removal coal mine to confirm that fact. But all of our lives tend to harm the Earth to some extent, both through unsustainable use of resources and unsustainable production of waste. To what harmful forces are we referring? From whom do we want to "save the Earth," and to what lengths are we willing to go to do so? Are we willing to do whatever it takes, or are the words empty talk?

When people speak or think of "saving the Earth," I don't believe they are necessarily invoking either of the possible meanings the phrase could hold. I believe those three words have morphed into a trite catchphrase with no real meaning except to advertise allegiance to some sort of "green" ideology. It does not mean the people who use the phrase or identify with the accompanying slippery ideology are any more likely to live sustainably than the average person. Their words are empty and carry neither understanding nor knowledge.

From a purely pragmatic perspective, the Earth does not need saving. It will, given time, survive any insult we heap upon it. It is we and the other current inhabitants of the planet who will suffer from the effects of our unsustainable lifestyle. We have both a moral and a practical duty to "save" (conserve and defend) the life currently populating this planet, but that's a different charge than what I believe most people have in mind when they speak of "saving the Earth." The difference is significant because it separates a true understanding of sustainability as an imperative from the superficial awareness most people have of the need to live in harmony with the systems of our planet. Just how shallow their cognizance is can be glimpsed in the glib mantra "save the Earth."

Flour Power

Being able to grow and process homegrown grain into homemade flour is an important step toward making your individual lifestyle a sustainable one. Ironically, flour seems like such a simple, basic item that most people take it for granted. But while lots of folks can grow a garden, very few can grow and process grain into flour.

If a grocery store is the only thing standing between your family and starvation, then you are in a very precarious predicament, maybe without realizing it. A social/economic collapse of the kind that will inevitably result from the unsustainable practices currently in play around the developed world will mean, among other things, empty store shelves. And while vegetables and fruit can be grown (and frozen or canned) and meat and fish can be raised or hunted (and frozen), a diet of only fruit, vegetables and meat is not something I would look forward to. Grain flour is the foundation of some very important dietary staples including bread, cereal, pasta and a whole host of baked goods.

This book is not a survival guide or how-to manual, but on the subject of grain and flour, a little background is in order. The grains most commonly used for flour are wheat, oats, rice, barley and corn. As long as hybrid varieties are avoided, all can be grown from seed saved from the previous year's harvest. The flour called for in most recipes is wheat. Bread flour (the best kind of wheat flour for bread) is made from varieties of wheat with a high protein content, also known as hard wheat. Cake flour (the best for cakes) is made from wheat varieties with low protein content, also known as soft wheat. All-purpose flour is a mix of high- and low-protein wheat and can be used for a variety of baking applications.

Wheat contains three parts: the endosperm (the soft inner part); the bran (skin); and the germ (seed). White flour uses only the endosperm. Whole wheat flour uses all three parts and is more nutritious and higher in fiber than white flour but goes rancid faster because of its higher oil content. If you attempt to grow and process grain for flour, don't expect the same delicious results as can be found in the plethora of baked goods available at a high-end grocery store. You'll never match the variety and sophistication of professional bakeries, which have access to complex leavening agents and other ingredients. Leavening or baking powder, which helps make baked goods rise by creating bubbles (of carbon dioxide) within the dough, can work at low temperatures, like yeast, or at high temperatures, like chemical agents such as calcium phosphates. Some chemical leavening agents work at both high and low temperatures, earning the title "double acting." A word about gluten: many health-conscious people avoid gluten, but there's no need unless you have a rare allergy. Gluten is a protein composite found in grains. It helps baked goods rise and makes them chewy rather than crumbly.

As mentioned, your baked goods won't turn out the same as those produced in modern bakeries. A glance at the ingredients of many will show items you could never hope to have access to in a post-industrial world. Some such ingredients include: alumina, or aluminum oxide; phosphoric acid; SAIP or sodium aluminum phosphate; and DATEM, and emulsifier made from tartaric acid and mono- and di-glycerides (fats) that improves the texture of baked goods by strengthening the network of gluten bonds in the dough. But even without fancy ingredients, you can definitely make some much-welcomed, flour-based additions to your diet. That know-how will be immensely valuable in the future.

You'll need a high-quality grain mill to grind your grain into flour. A manual mill is simplest and most reliable. Expect to spend a few hundred dollars for a grain mill worth owning. Next, spend a few years learning how to grow and process the grains needed for baking. Specialize in making your favorite grain-based foodstuffs and perfect your techniques.

Corn is easiest to grow and prepare because the ears are big. Just let them dry on the stalk and then break the kernels from the cob before grinding. Corn meal (ground corn) is easy to make and is the main ingredient in corn bread and corn muffins, which alone would go a long way in adding variety to a diet of vegetables and meat. Wheat is a little harder to grow (requiring two seasons for winter wheat, which is planted in the fall and harvested the following summer) and process (it must be threshed and separated from the chaff, both of which are somewhat tedious processes), but with wheat, you have the makings of some of the most useful flour in the world. Most people will probably want to focus on bread recipes as the main application for their wheat flour. Bread seems like a simple food. The old joke about bread and water being the mundane ration of inhumane prisons fails to consider what a tremendous addition basic bread would be to a diet made up only of other items you could grow or hunt yourself, without benefit of a grocery store.

Whether you enjoy producing and baking with your own flour as a hobby or merely want that skill set as an important part of a sustainable lifestyle, there's no denying the power of flour.

A Long Journey

Humans are somewhere in the early stages of a long journey. We started our trip down a path no other animal had ever taken when evolution gave our ancestors a knack for using tools and intelligence to make their lives both easier and more successful. By following this path, early humans cemented a very unconventional future for us, their progeny.

Think of nature and the natural interactions of all living things as an ocean. Instead of swimming in that sea with every other animal species, humans and human civilization are now riding atop it in a boat. We still need nature. After all, it's what supports us. But we are no longer in there, slugging it out to survive with our wild neighbors. From our current vantage point in the boat, we can see more than we ever could before. We have the unique luxury of pondering a system (the proverbial ocean of nature) that we are now sadly less a part of than we were before leaving on our journey. To gain the privilege of surveying the natural world, we have surrendered our membership and are now largely outsiders.

Modern society and our human lifestyles are very different from those of other animals, but despite the vast differences, our journey has just begun. We'll have to go much farther than we've come if we want our divergent path to lead us to a place as sustainable as the one we left. Wild animals must survive the elements and successfully hunt for food if they wish to survive. We humans live in climate controlled conditions (largely protected from the weather) and buy our food from stores (no hunting or gathering required). But for us, besting the elements and procuring food takes money, which we earn by working for a paycheck. So while wild animals struggle in the natural world, we struggle in the work world to achieve the same ends by different means, and as anyone who has felt the sting of a backstabbing, competitive workplace can attest, it can seem just as savage in its own way. If you don't have what it takes to survive, you will perish. Where's the humanity in that? What's the difference between our way and nature's way? If the journey we began at our birth as a species is really going to take us someplace new, we have a long way to go.

The term "civilized" suggests that we are more refined and gentle than the natural world, which mercilessly punishes any defect in one's ability to survive. Civilization implies compassion, and indeed humans have achieved some ability to show concern and caring for things other than themselves and their offspring. Religions tell us God loves all of creation and encourages us to do the same, within the limits of our abilities. Clearly, we are not there yet, but we seem more capable of empathy than any other animal on Earth. And if history is any indication, we are becoming more civilized, more humane with each passing century. This progression is important. That our compassion is exhibiting directionality hints that someday our society may be a place without scorn, discrimination, hatred or cruelty. Someday even cynicism and indifference may hold no place in a world filled with sincere kindness. A society in which people treated one another this well would also undoubtedly be one that would exude courtesy and concern for the natural world and everything that depends upon it—including future generations.

A truly sustainable lifestyle and a society at peace with itself and the planet would be a laudable destination for the long journey we began when we distinguished ourselves from the rest of life on Earth. I hope our destiny is that lofty and that our journey does not end up being a low road leading us to failure. From where we are now, it looks as if our prospects depend largely on our ability to embrace sustainability. Doing so would demonstrate we have caring hearts and would also give us the time we need to develop them to their fullest potential.

The Hard Way, The Easy Way, or The Right Way

There are three ways for humans to approach living on Earth—the hard way, the easy way or the right way. Early humans and their pre-human ancestors had no choice but to live the hard way. The hardships of subsistence living were the motivation for our obsession with making tools and developing technology. Over thousands of years of focusing on making every aspect of our existence easier, we perfected the lifestyle of convenience and luxury we enjoy today. We have unquestionably achieved ease of living, but in our pursuit of that singular goal, we have allowed all kinds of flaws to arise within the structure of the lifestyle we designed. These flaws are the many ways in which our individual, societal, industrial and governmental practices are unsustainable. Sooner or later these practices will fail because of the design flaws we overlooked while creating them. If our lifestyle were a machine, it would face numerous product safety recalls. These mistakes occurred because as we developed our modern lifestyles, our attention was focused only on achieving particular outcomes as quickly, easily, effectively, cheaply or profitably as possible. Often, the side effects of our developing lifestyles were not considered, particularly if those side effects did not or would not become problematic until sometime in the future. Such shortsightedness was not smart. Intelligent engineering anticipates how particular applications will perform over time, but we have not done that—yet.

It's time to re-examine everything we do, this time with the future in mind. Sustainability must be our first consideration. After all, if something is not sustainable, what good is it? How can we be satisfied with processes and practices we know are fatally flawed? We should feel driven to perfect our lifestyles by driving out unsustainable attributes and replacing them with modified approaches that will serve our needs but also last. We owe it to future generations to lay this groundwork for sustainable living. This new focus on sustainable living instead of instant gratification would be unprecedented in human history. Such a sea change would mark a new era in our existence as a species. Living the right way—sustainably—is the only responsible choice we have. Doing so will be a little less convenient and a little more expensive than the way we're living now, but it's the only viable option. Living responsibly and fulfilling one's obligations are always a little tougher than taking the easy way out, but it's always worth the effort. It's what separates lazy people from upstanding citizens. I, for one, want future generations to know I was prescient enough to see the need for sustainability and principled enough to actually strive for it. If everyone were so inclined, we could get down to the business of living the right way.

Strange Loyalties

At least 164 million Americans own pets, mostly domesticated dogs or cats, and they love them to an extent that is hard to describe and even harder to understand. Many pet owners sincerely consider dogs and cats to be members of their family. These are not lonely people who have no one to love. They have families, relatives and friends, but they are as emotionally attached to their dogs and cats as they are to their own children. Together, they spend about $60 billion a year on these animals. Despite a willingness to spend $60 billion on pets, Americans offer less than $5 billion in charitable contributions annually for wildlife conservation.

The culture of pet ownership is almost cult-like, and to not share people's fanaticism for these animals is perceived by many as heresy. But the question is, why? Despite the fact that many pet owners would risk their lives for their dogs or cats, they show little or no devotion or concern for wild animals. News of a dog or cat being abused or neglected will elicit from them an ire few offenses can match. Many find it physically sickening to think of a pet suffering. But these same people will drive right by (or live in) a housing development or strip mall being carved out of a woodlot without a thought or care for the suffering being meted out to the wildlife whose world is being torn apart with them in it.

Why Americans care so much about domesticated animals, which add nothing to the ecological richness of the Earth, but are so ignorantly ambivalent to native wildlife—the heart and soul of biodiversity on this planet—is frustrating and inexplicable. The domesticated animals they love so dearly contribute nothing to nature. They are not part of any ecosystem and have no role in the natural world. Cats, in particular, actually cause significant ecological damage, exerting unnatural predatory pressure on many important species of wildlife that are not adapted to withstand the additional losses. The nearly 80 million domesticated cats that live in the United States kill between 1.4 and 3.7 billion songbirds every year. That's a staggering loss that is surely contributing to population declines and even extinction among birds that are already experiencing habitat loss and competition from invasive species.

Many people seem to see no difference between wildlife and domesticated pets. Many claim to be "animal lovers," and as such profess to care for "all living things." Those sentiments are nice, but the "love" and "devotion" they heap on their domesticated pets come at a price to the Earth, which eventually results in detriment to the wild animals those people claim to also care about.

The $60 billion Americans spend on their pets every year pays for food, medicine and material items that require a lot of natural resources to produce and transport. Cat and dog food is just as expensive in terms of the resources needed for production as our own food. The meat and grain ingredients of pet food are agricultural products, just like our own food. Producing it takes the same toll on the land, air and water that producing our own food does. Pet food, of course, has to be processed and packaged, both of which take lots of energy and resources. Remember, every dollar of goods and services in our economy comes from the Earth, so Americans' pets tap the planet for $60 billion of its lifeblood every year. It's an extravagant waste of resources in an already very wasteful society. It adds significantly to the unsustainability of the social and economic house of cards we have built.

So let's trace the steps. First, precious natural resources are wasted to produce food for domesticated pets that contribute nothing to the natural world. These calories, vitamins and minerals sap nutrients that could otherwise enrich a natural ecosystem somewhere. Instead, the domesticated animals use the energy from this food to go out and harass or kill ecologically important animals, mostly songbirds, by the billions. Then, the only thing of value remaining from this tragic process—the rich bodily waste of these domesticated animals—is carried by a diesel-powered, exhaust-spewing garbage truck to a landfill where it will remain sequestered from the natural world for quite a while. As if to make this situation as bad as humanly possible, many pet owners put their pets' waste in plastic containers before sending it to ecological purgatory. And that's just food. There's a similar story for the medicine and material items produced, purchased and then discarded by Americans for domesticated pets in this country. Americans actually spend hundreds of millions of dollars each Halloween buying costumes for their dogs and cats. In 2014, they spent $350 million—an astonishing statistic that should simply speak for itself. Clearly, these people have priorities that do not include thrift or sustainability. That's a problem that cannot continue.

Do Americans love their pets so dearly because they are the only animals that will love them back? (Whether they really do or not is a subject of some debate.) Do humans possess some latent guilt about what we are doing to this planet—guilt that drives pet owners to seek absolution from another species of Earthly life, even domesticated life we've remade to our liking? Or maybe love of pets is human goodness, a benevolent virtue that like so much else about us is tragically out of alignment with the natural world and warped in a way as to make it unsustainable. Perhaps Americans' love of pets is proof that somewhere deep inside them lies an undeveloped ability to love the natural world as well. Like a child who loves his imaginary friend, maybe it's a developmental step leading to a well-adjusted state of maturity sometime in the future.

Anthropologists tell us that early humans formed an almost symbiotic relationship with wild dogs. Each benefitted from the protection and hunting talents of the other. Maybe people's obsession with dogs is somehow rooted in that part of our past. The early domestication of livestock was of great benefit to humans trying to figure out a transition from wild, subsistence living to a more comfortable, settled existence. Again, maybe the past lives on in us, explaining part of our affection, our preference for animals we "own" over wild animals that pay us no mind.

Regardless of the reasons, love of any kind is surely better than hatred or cruelty. And life, no matter what form it takes, is something good—something to be marveled at. If owning domesticated animals instills love and a respect for life in people, then that attribute can be counted as a positive. But one positive attribute does not make an entire system sustainable. America's current model of pet ownership is unsustainable. Like much of the rest of our lifestyles, it will need a serious makeover if we hope to avoid the unpleasant eventualities of unsustainable practices. Humanity can continue, but not this way. We should care as much about the health of our living Earth as we currently do about the welfare of our pets. Ironically, our strange loyalties and misguided priorities, which feel like love of animals to us, are taking us needlessly into a future of increased suffering and hardship for all life on Earth.

Embracing Sustainability

A Chance

Astronomy and physics are beginning to show us how amazing the universe is. Our precious Earth and the solar system that houses it are tucked away nonchalantly in a rather typical galaxy, one of many scattered across a vast firmament. We have learned just enough about the universe to know that it has many exotic secrets we won't be able to unlock until science advances significantly. The mysteries of the universe await us, but to solve them will require us to persist as a species long enough to do so. Extraterrestrial life, black holes, dark matter, dark energy, parallel universes, dimensions beyond those we can currently perceive, the relationship between space and time, subatomic particles, even time travel are among the concepts to which we will someday find answers of one kind or another. The age of discovery is just beginning! We have so much ahead of us, such a bright future full of excitement and promise. But we're in jeopardy of losing our chance. If, by failing to embrace sustainability, we destroy ourselves, we will lose not only what we now know, but everything we may someday know as well. We will lose a chance to see the mysteries of the universe revealed, and that would be a senseless shame.

Stars and planets are wondrous things—I can think of one of each I love very dearly. But space is not populated only with stars and planets, as we might think based on our own solar system. It is home to objects and phenomena so bizarre as to escape our ability to comprehend. We can only wonder and wait—wait for future generations to unlock these otherworldly truths. If one considers what we now know about the place we call space, it's hard not to believe that the mystery of life itself—its purpose, where it comes from and where it goes when we die—is locked up in the code of the universe. As we decipher the latter, the former will come into sharper focus, looming ever clearer until eventually, in an epic leap of wisdom, we have it. We may be a long way from that point, but we've made a good start. We have gained much more ground than any other species from this planet in pursuing the secrets of the cosmos. To lose it all because we were too weak or too undisciplined to demand sustainability from ourselves would be tragic. How could self-aware beings make such a mistake? How could we allow it? The time for a new renaissance, an awakening, is now.

We have a higher calling than engineering the next model year of pickup truck, producing the next season of a reality show or picking the winning brackets for the Super Bowl. We have better uses for our time than just killing time. We are here on Earth not just to exist, but to survive. We need to take our future seriously. Right now, we're coasting, running the clock out as is nothing mattered except making ourselves comfortable while we wait for the end. It's hard to focus on life's higher purpose amidst the distractions of day-to-day living—distractions that shorten our horizons and narrow our field of view. But we must. All life is driven to survive. Competition and self-preservation for the purpose of contributing to the future are the engines of evolution. We humans, because of the ways in which we are different from other animals on Earth, have unique responsibilities to the future. They include, among other things, solving the mysteries of the universe. We are the only inhabitants of this planet in a position to do so, and so we must. We must look for the clues in the cosmos that will answer the question, "Why are we alive?" We owe it to ourselves and to all living things to seek the answers. Remember that the next time you hear some politician mocking space exploration as a waste of taxpayers' money. We have a chance for true greatness. We have a chance at a future of enlightenment we can only imagine today. But carelessness can founder any ship. If we don't wake up and make provisions for the sustainability we'll need, the chance we've somehow been afforded will be lost.

Something to Fear

The current prominence of zombies and the zombie apocalypse in popular culture is not a coincidence or a meaningless trend. The fascination with zombie lore has arisen because on some level, people are feeling a sense of impending doom over their awareness that our society and our lifestyle are unsustainable in their current form. But instead of being able to confront their demons face to face, people conjure a mythical scapegoat, a fictitious proxy to both fear and hate. As an element of popular culture, zombies give people a common currency through which to communicate their fears. Zombies offer an acceptable way to express a shared understanding that a difficult struggle is looming, that the future does not look good, and that only those who prepare well stand any chance at survival. Desperation and hopelessness are prevalent themes.

No one truly believes our demise will come in the form of zombies stumbling toward us in a ceaseless quest to eat our brains, but finding an easily identifiable proxy to substitute for our fears is a very human practice. History is full of examples of people looking for a convenient vessel in which to house their fears. The gods, the stars, the devil, evil spirits, ghosts, witches, and more have all served this role. Given that our most current latent fears center around the problem of humans' own unsustainable lifestyles, it is probably not a coincidence that the scary thing we have conjured up to embody our fear is very human-like. Zombies not only look human, they are (or were) human before they die and cross over into a dark, desperate, hopeless lifestyle that cannot end well for anyone. They are damned to forever be the walking dead while we are doomed to be forever tormented by the mortal threat of becoming one of them—a fate worse than death itself. If you really think about the details of zombie mythology, it's uncanny how well it fits as a place for us to deposit our fears and dissonance over our current unsustainable way of life.

Zombie mythology portrays zombies to be terrible outsiders living among us, evil threats whose numbers are constantly increasing, drawing us closer and closer to an apocalypse. Not to belabor the obvious, but the apocalypse celebrated in zombie mythology is the end of our society, the end of our happy, comfortable, safe lifestyle. The notion of zombies closing in all around, surrounding us until there's no way out, is an allegory for the poison that oozes from an unsustainable society. The danger comes from others, but somehow, we deserve the mortal threat facing us. Something we are doing has put us in harm's way, and unless we quash that threat, it will overtake and destroy us. As portrayed in popular culture, zombies are totally evil and must be thoroughly vanquished. No one extends them any compassion, even in defeat. Our disdain for them is absolute. There is no way to coexist with zombies, no compromise or middle ground. They must either be destroyed, or they will destroy us. This aspect of zombie mythology represents a latent understanding that sustainability is an all-or-nothing proposition. We will either achieve sustainability or our society will collapse. There is no in-between.

In zombie mythology, it is possible that people we know or love could become zombies, forcing us to kill them or be killed. This part of zombie lore represents that very real struggle over resources that could arise during a societal collapse brought on by unsustainable practices. When food, water and items necessary for survival become critically scarce, people will do whatever they have to do to either obtain or defend them. This will pit people against people, possibly even friends and family against each other. Documented cases of cannibalism prove that people's instinct for self-preservation can overpower social bonds. Accessing resources could become a matter of life and death following a societal collapse. Roaming bands of survivors will be searching for what they need to survive. To those already in possession of vital resources, these people will seem like interlopers attempting to steal life itself. They will seem like zombies, relentlessly closing in from all sides. Just as in zombie mythology, people being threatened by outsiders attempting to compete over resources will have to either fight for those resources or flee. Depending on the circumstances, there may not be enough for everyone. Coexistence and survival may not be compatible. This is the worst-case scenario that seems to lie at the root of the zombie phobia that is increasingly present as an element of popular culture. Talk about latent fears. Psychologists could have a field day ferreting out all the parallels between society's fascination with zombies and dissonance over our unsustainable lifestyle. But as sometimes happens with our greatest fears, we hide behind denial. Many people will refuse to confront the issue of sustainability directly, instead focusing on the allegory of the zombie apocalypse. Doing so will probably prevent or delay meaningful action to fix the problem.

In zombie lore, the people most likely to survive are the ones who prepare well. Stockpiling food and weapons and hiding out in a secure location is seen as the key. Again, this reveals an awareness that in the future, resources will become scarce and survival will be a challenge. That's a pretty accurate parallel to what faces people when unsustainable living practices break down. But hoarding resources is not the answer, and waiting, as if for a storm to pass, won't help at all. Finding sustainable ways to meet our needs is the only way to remove the threat facing us. Zombies are no more real than werewolves or vampires, but until we embrace sustainability, we all have something very real to fear.

Parallel Comprehension

A city near which I live is apparently developing a permanent population of homeless people. I say apparently because several street corners and intersections have become regular spots for people asking for handouts. This has only been going on in this city for a couple of years or so. Prior to that, one would never have seen someone holding a sign beseeching passersby for money. I mention this because during the short time that panhandling has become highly visible in this town, the number of homeless people using one particular intersection rose steadily but then declined. The intersection in question was an ideal location for such an activity, with heavy traffic from two directions and long red lights. As such, it was the choice of the first panhandlers to begin soliciting on the streets of this city. But as the number of homeless people using the same intersection day after day continued to increase, their numbers reached some sort of saturation point, and the productivity of the spot dropped below what most of them considered worthwhile. Either by personally experiencing greatly diminishing returns or just by seeing the writing on the wall, most of the homeless people who had been using that intersection headed for other spots in town that had not been worked so heavily. In short, these people understood that continuous and increasing panhandling pressure on that particular intersection was not permanently feasible. Local residents who watched the homeless people disperse to other parts of the city understood the logic of it too. They understood something that required the same cognitive perspective necessary to comprehend sustainability. They could see why an unsustainable practice could not last, and they realized the need for an alternative. But despite this, most people seem blithely unaware of the concept of sustainability, as it is defined in this and similar works. Few know what it means, and even fewer appreciate what would be required to achieve it. But even as real understanding of sustainability remains elusive, our society is full of evidence that people readily comprehend lots of concepts that are logically parallel to the notion of sustainability. In addition to the example of homeless people radiating outward from an over-solicited intersection, here are some instances of sustainability-like concepts that are universally understood with little or no head-scratching whatsoever:

Engineers designing public projects such as bridges and overpasses know what is required for the structure to serve its intended purpose for a fixed set of time known as its serviceable life. They know that if they don't build it to meet those parameters, it could fail prematurely. Respectable engineers would never include a component that could not withstand the demands of the predicted use. They design the project to meet or exceed expectations so that it will not fall short. This engineering strategy requires an understanding of principles almost logically identical to sustainability. Ironically, even though engineers (and the general public) understand that buildings, roads and bridges must be built to withstand a predicted level of use over a known period of time, they seem unwilling or unable to apply the same strategy to building our society as a whole. The buildings, roads and bridges that they so meticulously and scientifically design to be successful are key components of our failure as a society to embrace sustainability. The way in which buildings, roads and bridges (and the rest of our infrastructure) are being made and used cannot possibly be continued for even another few hundred years without exhausting the pool of resources we will need forever. Understanding that should not be any harder than understanding that using weak steel or concrete will cause them to fall down. We feel a sense of duty, a moral obligation to make sure our bridges won't collapse, but we are unwilling to make similar provisions for our society as a whole.

Executives in the restaurant industry use research and demographic data to predict whether a given location is likely to support a particular restaurant. They understand that if the numbers are not right, the proposed restaurant will not be profitable and will fail. Without evidence that its business can successfully last, they will not invest in the new restaurant. This simple concept, which few people would struggle to understand, is logically similar to the concept of sustainability. Being able to see, in detail, what will and won't be feasible for the long term is necessary in the restaurant industry. It's also necessary for our society, but as it stands now, greater forethought and planning go into the corporate decision of whether to place a new McDonald's in a particular city than went into the creation of the city itself. Our society as a whole grows and evolves almost spontaneously, with little or no planning, even as many of the micro-elements thereof receive great scrutiny. There are a thousand eyes looking at details, but no one is watching the big picture.

Businesses of all sorts study the economic relationship between price and demand when deciding how much to charge for their products. They know that without the right price point, a product line won't achieve maximum profitability and might fail altogether. If they cannot make a profit at a price point the market will bear, they will not produce the product in question. This is basic economics that everyone understands, but the logic underlying it is fundamentally identical to that subtending a concept few people, including economists, seem to grasp: sustainability.

Endurance athletes understand innately the need to match their intensity and pace with the distance of their event. A 5-K (3.1 miles) demands speed that the same athlete could never maintain for a marathon (26.2 miles). Weather and terrain also affect how hard a distance runner can push. Hold back too much and you won't run your best race. Go out too hard and your finishing time will suffer even more. Runners understand instinctively the need to find the fastest pace they can sustain for the whole race. Many non-runners have no problem grasping this concept either. Anyone, runner or not, who can comprehend the relationship between pace and distance should be able to understand sustainability as well.

Doctors and their patients understand that people's weight, blood pressure, cholesterol, blood sugar and triglycerides must remain within certain parameters. If these measures exceed certain levels, real health problems, including death, can result. You just can't have out-of-control weight, blood pressure, etc. and hope to live a normal, healthy life. Most people just know this on such a basic level that awareness seems automatic. Even most of the people who don't successfully manage their health usually understand that they should and know the risk they run in failing to do so. The mental perspective necessary to grasp health care needs is not different from the kind of understanding needed to comprehend sustainability. Again, the question remains, why is one so widely understood while the other remains fuzzy at best?

Scientists with the CDC and the EPA determine the maximum concentrations of chemical contaminants that can be encountered without experiencing adverse health impacts. Usually expressed in parts per million (PPM) or parts per billion (PPB), exposure at concentrations higher than the limit is thought to make health problems possible or even likely. The idea that pushing beyond certain limits, particularly within certain periods of time, will result in unacceptable consequences is easily understood in many contexts. But sustainability, which parallels logically all of the examples given here, seems baffling and unfathomable to many people. They can't even begin to see why life as they're living it now cannot continue that way indefinitely. Raising awareness and public consciousness about the need to embrace sustainability at both the individual and societal level is the most important need we face. It may also prove to be one of the hardest to achieve.

The Illusion of Abundance

Our unsustainable use of technology has created an illusion of abundance. From the perspective of our current lifestyle, it looks and feels very much as if we have enough of everything. All the food, water, energy and material goods anyone could want are easily available. Not only does there seem to be enough, it seems as if there are no limits. If you buy all the milk on the grocery store shelf, they'll just put more out. If you leave your water faucet run for two days straight, your tap won't run dry. As long as you can pay the bill, you can use all you want. And so it goes. Everything we need or want seems to be available in limitless quantities. But it is not so. We create the illusion of abundance through processes that are, without question, unsustainable. Continuing them will hurt us badly in the long run. To see the stark difference between the illusion of abundance we have created and the reality of what resources exist in sustainable quantities, try going onto the land and living a subsistence lifestyle. Even a handful of humans will exhaust the resources in most areas surprisingly quickly. This is what forced pre-agrarian humans to live as nomads. Few places could support them for long, and so they moved constantly. With the technological ability to beat that problem came the absolute necessity of figuring out how to do it sustainably. But no one has yet attended to that critical point. To do so will be hard and complicated, but without a keystone, an archway cannot stand, and without sustainability, the otherwise elaborate scheme of human civilization will fail.

Another way to see through the illusion of abundance we have artificially created is to observe how hard wildlife must work to survive. They live on the same Earth we do, many times in close proximity to us. There are no natural resources available to us that aren't also available to them. They are tougher and better adapted than us, but they exist on a razor's edge, fighting a lean, mean battle of survival while we relax in the lap of luxury. What accounts for this difference? Our technology and artificial manipulation of resources has created for us an abundance, but it is a temporary abundance, and thus an illusion. Our current practices cannot be maintained indefinitely. They are destined to self-destruct. Animals living directly off the land have no choice but to exist in a way that's in balance with the available resources. The same rules apply to us, but we're cheating. We need to find a way to apply technology that does not create resource friction, so that our lifestyle can be both comfortable and sustainable.

Prisoners unto Ourselves

Have you ever wondered why repressed citizens like those of North Korea don't rise up and demand freedom? American colonists sluffed off the British for a lot less. The answer is more complicated than it would seem, and one need look no further than our own subjugation at the hands of industry to see why. A great deal of what Americans can do and cannot do, a great deal of the freedom of choice we have or don't have, is because of decisions made by corporations. Large, publicly traded companies that rely on the profits we give them are somehow able to decide what type of food we can buy and whether it will be packaged in needless plastic destined to end up in the guts of some marine organism or shore bird. They decide what shows we can watch on television and what TV stations we can have access to. They can make us pay for access to programming we don't want just to obtain what we do. And of course, they decide how much we have to pay. They can even compel us to sign contracts agreeing to continue buying the products they say we have to buy, whether we want to continue or not. Do these sound like the conditions of a "free market"? It depends on whose freedom you're referring to.

These corporations want to be left alone to operate as they see fit with no regulations or oversight. They don't hide the fact that they resent attempts to keep them from abusing their power. They complain vociferously about government regulation. Corporations will fight government, which represents us, the citizenry, in an attempt to smack down any effort to rein them in. By fighting government regulation, they are, in essence, fighting us, attempting to beat the American people into submission so that they can extract wealth from us without having to notice or care that their operations cause harm. If they could get away with even more, they would. The strange thing is, if we were in their shoes, most of us would do the same thing.

All this talk of people, government and corporations builds walls between these groups and creates the idea that they are separate. But in reality, they are not. Governments and corporations are made up of people, people who go to work for a living and then come home to live lives like everyone else. So all the abuses and offenses of government and industry are really just the actions of people interacting with other people. Is this how we want to act? Is this how we want to treat one another? Is a society whose behavior is based on greed and control a sustainable society? Could we change if we wanted to?

The strange sociology behind North Koreans' support of the totalitarian regime that represses them is the same as our support of the unsustainable practices we say are part of the American dream. We prefer the comfort of familiarity and the promise that tomorrow will be good, even if

Embracing Sustainability

it's easy to see that promise is a lie. Whether your oppressor is an eccentric dictator or the dysfunction of an unsustainable lifestyle, most people lack the courage to break free and march into a scary, unknown future to find a better way.

Awareness and Action: Still Disconnected

As president Obama neared the end of his second term, he began to speak more boldly about climate change and renewable energy. He spoke more blatantly than sitting presidents usually do, saying there's no doubt we have run out of time to procrastinate. Without real change now, future generations will suffer the un-mitigatable consequences of our choices. Yes, he's talking only about climate change caused by CO2 emissions and not the myriad of other sustainability related issues that are equally urgent, but still, his unequivocal assessment is refreshing in a world more often filled with platitudinous rhetoric. What's more, he's not alone. There seems to be a consensus growing around the same message Obama is preaching about climate change. This is how societal awareness begins. A few voices become many. Then, more prominent and more influential voices join the chorus until the message becomes mainstream. We may be undergoing that transformation now. It's easy to sense the growing awareness, the growing acceptance of the notion that climate change is real and that renewable energy will be the way of the future.

But equally as palpable is that there is a huge disconnect between awareness and action. Even as people come to admit the problem of CO2 emissions, the number who seem ready to do anything substantive about it is clearly still inadequate. Far too many seem to think—to wish—that the necessary actions will occur gradually, in good time, and at a pace that will not disturb the comfort of our current lifestyle. It's the same lack of true commitment that causes people to break New Year's resolutions. Without enough momentum to carry us from societal awareness to societal action, we may lose the coming chance for another generation.

And remember, all the attention is for now focused on climate change, which is frankly one of the easier obstacles standing between us and sustainability. Many people have already beaten the carbon demon in their own lives, powering their homes entirely with solar panels and driving electric vehicles that they also charge using homegrown power. Becoming carbon neutral or even carbon negative is ridiculously easy compared with the struggle we will face in achieving sustainability in our consumption of other natural resources and in our production of other wastes and pollutants. But hey, we're innovators, and we enjoy the challenge of solving problems in order to make our lives better. We certainly have such a challenge before us now. Embracing sustainability is imperative for our species' survival, and we have a lot of work to do in pursuit of a lifestyle that can last.

Where the Wild Things Are

From the time they are babies, American children are subjected to a barrage of messages that suggest exotic wildlife from faraway places or a different time are more important than animals from their own ecoregions. Dinosaurs are portrayed as the ultimate in exciting, interesting animals. Even though they've been extinct for millions of years, they seem to rank as the most popular animals among young children. They are celebrated with toys, games, TV shows, books, movies, clothing, costumes and more, and lots of kids know the names of more dinosaurs than of animals that might show up in their own backyard today. 65 million years since they disappeared, dinosaur mania reigns in American popular culture. I wonder if we humans will be as popular among the future inhabitants of this planet?

Even though dinosaurs went extinct naturally, they are celebrated in ways more contemporary species driven to extinction by human avarice are not. Childhood and dino lore just seem to go together, but how many kids are as well versed on the dodo, great auk or passenger pigeon? What have we taught our children about these extinct animals, and what does the answer say about our culture and our priorities?

Of currently living animals, lions, tigers, elephants and similar megafauna of Africa or Asia are portrayed as most worthy of attention. And while they certainly are worthy, the unfortunate implication of all the emphasis they receive is that wildlife one might see in a typical American backyard is not. The typical American grade-school student can probably name more African animals than North American animals. Children who grow up with this worldview turn out to be adults who believe conservation is some vague concept to somehow be applied in exotic places like rainforests. But if a few hundred acres of local forest is targeted for "development," they see nothing of particular value in jeopardy. Local ecosystems, many of which are more diverse than faraway ones, are perceived as "vacant, overgrown land," "scrubland," "swamps," "brush," or other epithets revealing the belief that a bulldozer is probably the best thing that could happen to those "neglected" places.

Much is written in the areas of education and psychology about the importance of ensuring young children are exposed to the right messages. The learning that takes place during early development is the most important because this is when the major wiring of children's brains is being programmed. What a convoluted appreciation of life on Earth we cultivate when the earliest messages about wildlife involve creatures most kids will never see. For them, even as adults, conservation and sustainability remain nebulous concepts applied only in faraway, imaginary places where the wild things are.

Sustainability Is Morality

The most obvious reasons for pursuing sustainability are pragmatic ones. But there's a philosophical reason as well—it's simply the right thing to do. The Earth's purpose in the universe is greater than that of a vessel for life. Much of this book argues that our actions should promote life and preserve biodiversity because the planet will be a richer place as a result. But the purpose of life on Earth is more than biological. The universe (or multiverse as physicists now suppose) is governed by forces and laws we don't understand. Somehow, those forces and laws have conspired to create the Earth we know, replete with the splendid array of life it harbors. Who are we to second-guess or disrespect this plan by defiling it? Yes, we should be concerned that the natural balance of the Earth's ecosystems remains intact, but not just so we can continue to enjoy the blessings they provide. Our reasons for caring about sustainability should include a reverence for creation and an ethically based sense of obligation to do the right thing. To disregard the future and dismiss any duty to choose right over wrong is to align oneself with another force that exists in the universe—entropy, the dark force of disorder, death and destruction.

Religions universally include the notion that good should be chosen over evil and that doing so will please the creator. Morality and choosing right for right's sake are widely understood to be the path of righteousness. Accepting this notion as a given and working from it, it is easy to justify the pursuit of sustainability solely because it is the right thing to do. Creation is a wonder. We ought to be in awe of it and regard it with reverence and respect. Too often, people who disagree with sustainability-related measures insist we provide some practical reason why we should care about or need to conserve the natural world. A whole class of rhetorical constructs related to "ecological services" has arisen to answer their demands and attempt to explain for them why we should behave in a way that shows we care for the Earth and the living systems it houses. But like telling rebellious children that it really matters that they do their homework and brush their teeth, it is obvious critics are seldom fully convinced by these arguments. Despite the protestations of those to whom sustainability seems an inconvenience, no justification is necessary. A moral person perceives the wrong in gluttony, largess and living less honorably that we know how to or are capable of. Right is right, and good is good, and neither requires explanation. The values inherent to both sustainability and morality create their own worth. In that way, sustainability is morality.

Kindness Is Sustainable

Occasionally I am struck by how relatively primitive our human actions and ideology are. In comparison to what they might someday become, our current approaches to living and interacting with one another are very low on the developmental continuum. A sense of humanity, empathy and altruism set Homo sapiens apart from other animals, but we still have tremendous room for growth in those areas.

People have dreamed of peace for ages, and we are in many ways more civilized than our ancestors. But consider how common war, crime and abuse are. I believe that if we ever do achieve sustainability, we will find that a profoundly greater sentiment of humanity, a sense of kindness, will accompany it.

Nature is hard and unforgiving. We ran that gauntlet for millions of years until evolution set us on a path that eased the fierce hardship of wild living. We now feel that there is a fundamental difference between us and our wild brethren. We call that difference civility—the trappings of civilization. But our current civilization is neither kind nor sustainable. We are still in transition—at some point along the continuum between wild and something better. Perhaps that something better is the next plateau in social evolution. If we are moving progressively from a wild state to a civilized one, maybe we humans will be the first beings on Earth to achieve a level of development that includes the display of pure kindness and compassion.

Sustainability is a crossroads—a tipping point between living and dying, succeeding and failing. We are a long way from ensuring that we make it. Our unpreparedness takes many forms, including our incomplete humanity, our partial civility. Perhaps if we learn to live in balance with the resources of this planet, we will also learn to live in harmony with one another. Perhaps if we succeed in making the leap to the next level of social evolution and achieve sustainability, we will find that it is automatically accompanied by a more perfect capacity for beneficence. Perhaps kindness will become sustainable.

The Media and Sustainability

The mainstream media, by which I mean the entertainment, advertising and especially news media, are doing a great disservice to efforts to raise public awareness of the need to achieve sustainability. This is because most of the content in the media reinforces the notion that our society is basically OK the way it is. News programming should be full of reports sounding alarm bells over the unsustainable lifestyle we have constructed, but they aren't. Instead, the majority of what gets covered contains nothing about sustainability. Sustainability (or unsustainability) is woven into every aspect of our society, all parts of our individual lives. Therefore, the potential for it to be a part of most matters covered by the media is there. Every story and every topic contain elements that relate to sustainability on some level. But just as most people are blind to sustainability in their daily lives, so are our media blind to sustainability in most of what they cover, even when it is right before them.

The future of human civilization is not a "story" or an "issue." It is, or should be, an imperative that guides our lives. It should be present, included, considered in all we do. In the days and weeks following Sept. 11, 2001, few stories did not contain some shadow of the terrorist attacks. Not just the obvious stories covering the attacks and their aftermath, but all stories. Stories about a baseball game or a city council meeting contained some dimension that was related to the events of Sept. 11. It was, at the time, all-consuming. If sustainability were to occupy its rightful place in our collective psyche, it would be as omnipresent as our instinct for self-preservation, our love for our children.

Some media content addresses sustainability, but rarely adequately, and the fact that most such content is greatly outnumbered by content that doesn't consider sustainability suggests to the public that the status quo is acceptable. The media imply that concern about sustainability should be compartmentalized into a realm that is understood to be subordinate to the regular order of things. This marginalization of sustainability creates a narrative that says concern about sustainability should remain a secondary perspective, an outlier mentality, an alternative ideology that does not deserve or need to become a primary concern for mainstream society. Don't underestimate how influential this lack of attention to sustainability is. It really does cement in people's minds the notion that nothing is wrong with how we are going about living on this planet (or at least not wrong enough to be worried about).

Some say that for the media to intentionally champion an "issue" such as sustainability would be to abdicate the respected tradition of journalistic objectivity. The media should not be crusaders, conventional wisdom asserts. In this line of thinking, objectivity is perceived as the absence of bias. It is the opposite of subjectivity, which tells only one side of a two-sided controversy. But this perception of the media and their role is naïve. It ignores the reality on the ground. What a dogmatic allegiance to journalistic objectivity fails to recognize is that it's impossible to be "objective." It's impossible to tell a story and not endorse some perspective on the matter being covered. For many matters, including sustainability, coverage that seems to make no endorsement or offer no guidance sends a message of apathy. Such coverage suggests that not taking a position is a viable option. It says not caring is OK. Sending such a message, intentionally or not, most definitely takes a side. If no urgency is suggested, the take-away is that business as usual is a safe, comfortable choice. And so by trying to be "objective" and not actively promote sustainability, media outlets are actually taking the side of the status quo, which is, of course, an unsustainable lifestyle that endorses all of the behaviors and practices that are so problematic for our long-term survival.

Changing the media to embrace sustainability in all they do may seem like a monumental task, a massive makeover of an institution whose current manifestation seems incapable of conforming to this new normal. But if public attitudes would shift significantly enough, the change could happen with surprising ease. How might public attitudes change this much? Well, given the media's ability to inform public opinion and set the agenda for social discourse, getting ahead of the curve on progressive social issues puts the media in the position to be drivers rather than followers of positive social change. It's called advocacy journalism. By beginning to cover sustainability with more prominence and urgency, the media could be the agents of their own change. But the media are not currently leading us toward a sustainable existence. Instead, they are issuing a daily drumbeat of rhetoric that is keeping us chained to our current ways, preventing us from changing quickly or at all.

Two of the most esteemed functions/duties of the mass media are truthtelling and social responsibility. These mean that the media have an indelible obligation to tell the truth and to champion whatever is in the best interest of society. Well, the truth (which the media aren't telling) is that our society is doomed unless we embrace a sustainable way of life. Working to avert the collapse of human civilization is the greatest opportunity to fulfill their social responsibility the media will ever face. That most journalists feel uncomfortable doing so, as if it is not their place to fight that battle, is more evidence that we don't have a clear view of the world in which we live or the real challenges facing us.

Sustainability and Education

Our educational system, like our political and media systems, is badly broken. It does not work well at all and falls far short of delivering the most valuable of all possible educational outcomes—citizens who respect what is right, cherish morality, value what is virtuous, understand it's important that we leave the world a better place than we inherited, yearn for a sustainable society and know what it takes to achieve these things. Instead, we have an awkward system that inefficiently imparts a few basic skills such as how to read, write and count and then sends graduates stumbling into a world they have never really gotten to know. Many of the college students I've encountered in 15 years of teaching at various universities are barely literate and intellectually stunted. I can't help but wonder just what they've been exposed to in their first couple of decades of life. Clearly not the right things, for most are utterly clueless.

The American educational system is a powerful force in maintaining the status quo and conditioning generation after generation of kids to see the world from an anthropocentric perspective. Children spend most of their lives in school, where the one overarching message of all their classes seems to be that humans and the dysfunctional society we have built, seemingly without a plan of any kind, are all that matter.

History classes are perhaps the worst offenders. The only history that is taught is the history of human activities. Human wars and political events are the staple of these classes. American history, from the time of Christopher Columbus until today, includes the lessons we all learned about the Revolutionary War, the beginning of our nation, the Constitution and early presidents, the War of 1812, the Civil War, prohibition, the Great Depression (no lessons here about the dangers of unsustainable growth) World War 1 and World War 2 (the massive industrial underpinnings of which are touted as having saved our economy as surely as the atomic bomb saved us from our enemies). We have made sure no detail is omitted from these ubiquitous and familiar chapters of history.

But history classes make no mention of events or conditions that don't fit the anthropocentric definition of what's important. Forgotten are details about such matters as the great fisheries of the Atlantic Ocean that Columbus' Nina, Pinta and Santa Maria literally arrived upon. Imagine coastlines so teeming with life that a net cast anywhere may well break under the load. Those seemingly inexhaustible fisheries have since collapsed and don't seem to be coming back anytime soon. In many parts of the ocean, you are today more likely to find garbage than fish. The mindless overfishing of the 20th century should never have been allowed to happen, but no lessons to this effect are taught in our schools.

Also conspicuously absent from history curricula is much mention of the great forests of the Eastern United States that greeted the colonists and the pioneers they became as they pushed the frontier. When mentioned at all, the forests are described as significant obstacles to exploration and settlement. And while attention is given to the Native American culture that existed before Europeans arrived in the New World, little is said of the wildlife to be found there. Elk, bison, wolves, and mountain lions were all common in the Eastern United States when the Treaty of Paris was being signed. Which do you consider more interesting, more important?

And while not as exotic as the wooly rhinos, giant sloths, mammoths and saber-toothed tigers present here during the Pleistocene, the mega fauna of the New World represent just the highlights of wild ecosystems rich with intricate details and complex relationships, many of which are now gone forever. When foresters or dendrologists want to understand the forests that existed in the Eastern United States at the time of its discovery, they have to resort to such pathetic measures as analyzing the first property deeds issued for tracts of land being settled then. You see, the parts of the deeds that spelled out the boundaries for those parcels often relied on declaring that the property line would begin at, say, the stump of a large white oak and then commence in a southwesterly direction 150 rods to a pair of birch trees and then west to a dogwood. By the decidedly imprecise method of counting the frequency with which certain tree species were mentioned in property deeds, modern scientists can get a rough idea of the composition of the forests present when the East was settled. Despite the advances of modern science, it's the only way they can determine this because no one bothered to write any of it down or to keep records about the natural wonders that lay at the feet of early explorers. In many ways, we know as much about the land of the dinosaurs as we do about the land we built America on just a few hundred years ago. No one cared then, and judging by where we focus our attention today, that indifference seems to remain. Perhaps if we taught our children to care, the next generation could have better priorities.

Textbooks love to detail the adventures of Lewis and Clark, but little time is spent discussing the duo's discovery of prehistoric remains that helped to raise the concept of extinction into acceptance. President Thomas Jefferson, who sent Lewis and Clark on their expedition, was obsessed with the animals being found in fossils of his day. He held out great hope that living specimens of them might still roam the unexplored Western parts of the continent. Prior to the 1800s, even scientists doubted that extinction was real. People believed every species that had ever lived still existed and that none would be or ever could be lost. But as more fossils and other remains were discovered, it became impossible to ignore the evidence. Even a familiar signer of the Declaration of Independence (Jefferson) was deeply involved in this natural history renaissance, but it's a side of him we're not taught in school. The realization that extinction was real may be the most recent example of the population at large accepting irrefutable scientific evidence that contradicted their worldviews and violated their comfort zones. We're desperately overdue for a repeat, this time with the concept of sustainability. The school system could help, but has so far not offered much assistance.

The Civil War, which came to a head in the 1860s, is heavily discussed in American history classes, with some of the most somber lessons being about the need to learn from the past so as not to repeat our mistakes. These same classes make absolutely no mention of what was happening to the passenger pigeon in America at the same time as the Civil War, even though that sad chapter in history offers us similar lessons of even greater scope and severity. Does it seem right to you that one tragic tale of 19th century bloodshed is common while another is unknown?

The American educational system tells our children that the 1930s was a period of time between two world wars that featured such memorable events as the Great Depression and the end of prohibition. Perhaps a quick reference is made to an event known as the Dust Bowl, but students are not challenged to ponder it the way Aldo Leopold did. Unsustainable agricultural practices caused the most productive topsoil in the nation to literally blow away in the drought-stoked winds. The human misery resulting from this unnatural disaster is what gets the most attention, and if it weren't for this human element, the Dust Bowl might not be remembered at all. Nobody tells our children how that topsoil was formed to begin with. No one explains the native grassland regimes of switchgrass, big bluestem and Indian grass that swayed in the prairie breeze for millennia before the wagons and plows came. Nobody mentions prairie chickens or bobolinks or fringed orchids or why these living things, once plentiful, are now rare. No one admits that to feed millions, American farmers didn't have much choice. And certainly, nobody tells our kids that unsustainable agricultural practices of another kind still plague the heartland of America or that when these new mistakes backfire, the consequences will be farther reaching and longer lasting than the Dust Bowl.

In neither history nor science, sociology nor civics are America's children taught that the Ogallala aquafer, an underground oasis with as much fresh water as Lake Huron, is going dry so that vast agricultural monocultures may flourish. A Nebraska farmer trying to tap the Ogallala must dig deeper by about two feet each year. Wells that were productive in 1940 are now high and dry by more than 100 vertical feet, and some farmers already find it impossible or impractical to pull water up from the ever falling top of the aquafer. If we keep going it will be dry within a generation. If we stopped sucking the lifeblood from under the prairies today, rainfall would naturally recharge the Ogallala—in about 6,000 years. Might this be worth knowing?

Students are made to learn the capitals of all 50 states in social studies. They should not memorize this information without also being made aware of how fleeting such things are on nature's timeline. Our contrived geographical boundaries seldom match the ecological ones nature has assigned to the various landforms and climate zones, which too shall change, but only after eons of time scour and reorganize the face of the continent. Our land-use practices, by contrast, are sudden and violent, having jolted entire ecoregions of North America into new realities that neither the land nor its inhabitants could possibly hope to adapt to. The result has been erosion, flooding, pollution, decreased nutrient cycling and a loss of biodiversity.

10,000 years from now, knowing that Madison and Lincoln had long ago been the capitals of regions previously known as Wisconsin and Nebraska will seem an utterly irrelevant piece of information. What will have seemed far more worth teaching will be an appreciation of how glaciers and forests slowly waltz to and fro across the Eastern half of the continent while the Rocky Mountains, still thrusting skyward, cast a rain shadow that keeps the central portion in a tree-starved grassland regime. An amazing cast of plant and animal species follows like worshippers on pilgrimage, trailing these geologically derived conditions as they morph across the face of the land. But this is not what schools teach our children. Instead, they learn one or two key industries for each state—coal for West Virginia, cattle and oil for Texas, logging and fishing for Maine. They are told these pursuits are the foundations of these areas, important and enduring staples. No one confesses that these are unsustainable assaults that have beaten the true character of the land into retreat.

The educational system also fails to help our children realize the severity of the problem posed by invasive species. Non-native plants and animals now fill the world around us and would make it nearly impossible to recreate the oceans, forests or prairies that existed when Columbus arrived in the New World. Some of the first invasives probably came with him and his entourage. The rest trickled in with waves of explorers and immigrants who came to this continent over the succeeding centuries, but despite being part of every chapter of the American story, historians don't include invasive species in the lessons that form our children's understanding of what's important.

No child should graduate high school without learning their local flora and fauna. An educated person should be familiar with the identities and natural histories of the trees, plants, birds, fish, mammals, amphibians and reptiles that share their world. They should also get a healthy dose of entomology, learning a fair bit about the invertebrate world, especially the organisms that contribute to and support the production and function of healthy soil. Just the act of learning to identify the life around us would carry an important message: if it's worth learning about, it's worth caring about. It has value. The current educational system places no value on these things, so it's little wonder that the products of the educational system (most adults) don't either. The people who do value the natural world mostly come to hold that worldview because of some influence other than the school system.

By not teaching children about the natural world, we are really sending the message that it doesn't matter. It's little wonder many adults would think nothing of seeing 100 acres being cleared for the construction of houses or a shopping center. They literally don't know what's being lost. They don't know its value is greater than what it is being replaced with because they have never been told or shown.

Schools have had to fight to teach evolution (some are still fighting). A little bit of education encouraging kids to recycle or reduce energy consumption is about all that can be done without being accused of using the schools to brainwash kids with liberal, tree-hugger propaganda. It's a shame that respecting the Earth is a controversial position, that wanting a healthy planet is offensive to some. Politics has poisoned what should be a universally acceptable concept and neutered our schools' ability to teach it.

I think many Americans sense a void in our educational system. The idea that "they don't teach the most important things in school" is a timeless maxim that's more valid today than ever. I suspect few people really know why they feel that way or understand what's missing in our schools.

Do we dare tell our children what their parents and grandparents have done to the future they will inherit? American educators seem to think not. Instead they occupy our kids' minds, as if for purposes of distraction, with anthropocentric information that will matter little 500 years into the future. History teachers tell our children that it's important to learn from the past, but then omit the most important lessons. The overwhelming result of what is taught and what it not is that children come to believe war and politics matter but that issues related to the natural world such as conservation and sustainability do not. Can't we do better than that?

There Is No Sustainable Development

There is no such thing as sustainable development. Human alteration of the Earth's surface has already been sufficient to thrust our planet into a new geologic epoch—the Anthropocene. Additional human infrastructure of any kind if definitely not sustainable. Despite this, the absurd concept of sustainable development remains widely touted and much discussed by people who should know better.

The "millennium development goals" adopted by the United Nations in 2000 have expired, and the UN General Assembly just replaced them with "sustainable development goals" for the next 15 years. Many of the goals overtly contradict principles plainly inherent to sustainability, but hey, it's a catchy title, so the leaders of the most advanced nations on Earth ran with it. Among the dangerously misguided goals the UN has proffered under the misnomer of sustainability is to see the economies of many nations on Earth grow by 7 percent every year until 2030. This would result in them more than doubling in just 15 years! Who could think such a thing to be sustainable? This myopic goal is the result of the collective wisdom of the brightest, most progressive nations on Earth! If the future of the planet weren't at stake, such incompetence might be laughable.

In all, there are 17 main goals and 196 sub-goals in the UN's plan. Basically, the goals call for everyone on Earth to enjoy living standards similar to those "developed" nations such as America know today while at the same time stopping climate change, ending pollution, halting the loss of biodiversity and ensuring that the Earth's terrestrial and aquatic ecosystems are no longer imperiled by human activity. OK, want to guess how that'll work out? What a joke. Maybe we should be glad that they're at least paying lip service to sustainability, but until world leaders and industry get serious about ensuring humanity exists 1,000 years from now, we are really no better off at all.

Human infrastructure and economic growth are not "development." They are the unsustainable utilization of natural resources. "Development" is what evolution accomplished during the millions of year it took for life to spring from simple primordial elements into the complex diversity that adorned the Earth when the industrial revolution began. What we have done since then is to diminish, not advance, development. Sustainable development is more than a myopic misnomer, it is an obscene oxymoron that abets the ignorance of our leaders and allows us to deceive ourselves into thinking our future is bright.

Embracing Sustainability

The Right Side of the Road

Proof of people's ability to cooperate, work together and follow a set of agreed-upon rules is as easy to find as the nearest two-lane road. That millions of cars and trucks drive many more millions of miles every day is testament to more than our willingness to pollute our atmosphere for convenience and profit. It underscores the fact that when we all recognize the benefit of doing something, we can act with surprising unity of purpose. I am referring to how almost all drivers obey traffic laws so closely as to make sharing the roads a highly effective yet very basic occurrence. The practice of driving on the right side of the road (at least in America) is an especially good case in point. Clearly, it works. How many cars pass you going the other way on two-lane roads every day? Doubtlessly plenty, perhaps more than you can count or remember. How often are you involved in head-on collisions because drivers don't stay on their side of the road? Most people have never had this type of accident, despite driving every day. Head-on collisions rarely happen to us because most drivers follow the rules and thereby work together to make the system work.

Most people don't trust strangers. Few would allow a complete stranger to enter their homes, but when we are driving on a two-lane road, we trust countless strangers with our very lives. We count on them not to swerve into our lane and hit us head-on at speeds that would kill or seriously injure us. Why? Because if we didn't, our entire transportation scheme would be unworkable. And so we work together, follow rules we all agree are mutually beneficial, and trust one another to do the right thing. We all participate, and by doing our individual parts, we ensure the system will work.

If we wanted to embrace sustainability as much as we want to drive our cars, we could. If the same collective motivation to follow a universal set of rules that enables driving to work existed for ensuring our long-term survival, our progress and success in that area would be stunning. If we wanted to make humanity sustainable as much as we want to make driving feasible, we would already have achieved that goal. But instead, there is only a small minority willing to strive for sustainability. Most people are not on board, not participating. The masses do not share a common motivation, and so there is no unity of purpose. Sustainability will not be achieved through the fervor of a few, but through universal acknowledgement that it's something we all need to survive. If only 10 percent of drivers were willing to obey the rules of the road while the other 90 percent refused to do so, transportation as we know it would be impossible. We're all so accustomed to driving on the right side of the road that we take it for granted. We are blind to the power of cooperation, but proof that it exists is right in front of us every time we get behind the wheel.

Individualism Is Not Sustainability

People unfamiliar with the concept of sustainability sometimes think that someone who wants to live sustainably is attempting to live "off the grid," to be "independent" of society or "self-sufficient," needing nothing civilization has to offer. They assume someone who values sustainability seeks to set himself apart from society and live a hermit-like existence, eschewing technology and divorced from modernity. That stereotype is largely inaccurate. The skills possessed by survivalists and doomsday preppers may be useful in short-term emergency situations, but they are not equivalent to or substitutes for sustainability. No individual, regardless of his or her skills or level of preparedness, can exist indefinitely without the benefits of an organized society. Even if an individual of extraordinary physical toughness and exceptional resourcefulness could find and make all of his or her own food, clothes, shelter and tools with nothing but bare hands and raw materials from nature, that individual would not be a functional part of humanity. That person's isolation and non-participation would render him or her an outlier, not a productive member of society. A sustainable society will require its members to work together. Individuals living separate, unconnected lives would not make a sustainable society.

The main differences between a sustainable society and the one we have now are 1) population level and 2) the shared goals we are striving for. The society we have now is grossly overpopulated, and its goals focus mainly on the instant gratification, greed, comfort and convenience of its current members. A sustainable society would be one with a population that was but a fraction (1 percent or less) of our current seven billion. The goals of this sustainable society would be to ensure all future life on Earth would have what was necessary to flourish. Those are the linchpins of a sustainable society—a right-sized population living right.

Striving for sustainability in the midst of our current predicament can make it feel as if one needs to be the consummate individualist, a survivor going it alone. But that's not how it is. It only seems that way because seeing life through the lens of sustainability probably means no one you know shares your vantage point. But when and if humanity achieves sustainability, it will be a collaborative endeavor with the same specialization of labor and integration of individual skills and roles our current society is built upon. We'll all still be working together, just for different goals.

So whether you consider yourself an opinion leader, vanguard or early adopter of sustainability, remember that you will be alone in setting the example for others to follow, but that doesn't mean sustainability is about individualism. It is not. Nor is sustainability about "prepping." You can't hoard your way to sustainability because stockpiling commodities of any kind is not a permanent, renewable way of meeting your needs (unless those commodities are sustainably produced, in which case there would be no need to stockpile them). For example, sustainability will definitely involve making use of local food, including any you can procure for yourself. But canning supplies (jars, lids, bands, gel, sugar, etc.) are not things you can make yourself. Likewise, a refrigerator and freezer for food storage and a stove for cooking are items that must come from an organized society. No individual can produce these items alone, and living without such tools is neither necessary nor desirable. A society that produces useful commodities from renewable resources using sustainable processes for a properly sized population is a smart and prudent model. In no way are total individualism or doomsday prepping part of that picture. To blend a couple of common quotes, the Earth is our island home, but no man is an island unto himself.

Beyond Sustainability—Striving to Contribute as Planetary Citizens

What do we humans contribute to the Earth? How does our existence benefit the big picture of life on this planet? Unlike wild plants and animals, we humans take much more than we give in the balance of life. While other life forms contribute to the surplus of resources on the Earth, we deduct from that balance. Our existence is a net negative, a downward force on an equation that is trying to remain balanced or in positive territory.

We bring arts, intelligence and self-awareness. These are intriguing attributes that are intrinsically valuable because of their apparent scarcity. But that does not excuse us from living right. We should be striving for positive productivity as planetary citizens. Living sustainably means simply that we won't run ourselves into the ground by depleting resources we depend upon. Ideally, we could do more than just live sustainably. It would be nice if we could actually give back in a way that exceeds the value of what we deduct.

For instance, the invertebrates that live in the soil beneath our feet have, together with plants and fungi, built that soil up over millennia. Yes, they take some things from it to live, but in the course of that living, they give it all back and more. Their lives are a service that adds to, not deducts from, the soil resource. Higher up the chain of life, vertebrates from mice to deer also borrow from the soil bank to live their lives, but they pay back the debt as their waste and even their bodies return to the Earth upon death. They also pay interest in the form of ecological services such as seed dispersal and acting as prey species for all sorts of predators that add to the diverse tapestry of life on Earth. Even the top predators give back more than they take by keeping population levels of prey species in check and by exerting selective pressure that keeps prey species sharp and strong. Those services are very valuable. Virtually all life on Earth except humans can correctly claim to not only exist sustainably, but to actually add to a surplus of resources accruing as life marches on.

Living sustainably means, among other things, not using resources faster than they can be produced. But that can be done without adding anything to the system. If everyone else is producing a surplus of resources, the minimum requirements of sustainability include not subtracting resources faster than they are being added. In a productive ecosystem, it is even possible to be sustainable while operating as a net negative, as long as everyone else is productive at a rate that exceeds your negative impact. But is that what we want to be—dead weight on the backs of an ecosystem that pays the bills for our largess? How splendid would it be if we humans could join the ranks of plants and animals that actually contribute more than they take? Our intelligence and technological cunning give us a chance to serve Earth's ecosystems in a way no other species can. Mostly though, we would do well to just clean up the discordant lifestyle we've made for ourselves. After all, what impact can humans claim to have had on the Earth's ecosystems? Well, we've ushered in the planet's sixth mass extinction. In an astonishingly short period of time, we have managed to foul the air, water and soil over large tracts of the world. To power a frivolous, ecologically deadbeat lifestyle, we are burning through stored carbon that took millions of years to accumulate. And on and on it goes. Our legacy and performance are shameful, and yet many are proud of what they perceive to be our accomplishments as a species—feats no other species has ever matched. Far preferable to that dubious distinction would be to join the ranks of the many other species that not only live sustainably but contribute more in ecological services than they collect.

Embracing Sustainability

Copyright Permission Acknowledgements

Thanks to all the copyright holders who allowed their work to be reproduced here. They are:

Amsel, Sheri.	Wood frog
Feenix Publishing.	Milk Snake, Copyright Feenix Publishing
Goldfarb, Jack.	Northern red salamander
Gould, Anita.	Io moth
Hancock, J.D.	"Apple Earth" front cover photo
Harding, James H.	Gray treefrog

Houghton Mifflin Harcourt Publishing. Illustrations from A FIELD GUIDE TO WILDFLOWERS OF NORTHEASTERN AND NORTH CENTRAL NORTH AMERICA by Roger Tory Peterson and Margaret McKenny. Copyright © 1968 by Roger Tory Peterson and Margaret McKenny, renewed 1996 by Virginia Marie Peterson. Reprinted with permission of Houghton Mifflin Harcourt Publishing Company. All rights reserved.

Illustrations from A FIELD GUIDE TO MAMMALS OF NORTH AMERICA, 4/E by Fionna A. Reid. Copyright © 2006 by Fionna A. Reid. Reprinted with permission of Houghton Mifflin Harcourt Publishing Company. All rights reserved.

Illustrations from A FIELD GUIDE TO FRESHWATER FISHES OF NORTH AMERICA NORTH OF MEXICO by Lawrence M. Page and Brooks M. Burr. Illustrations copyright © 1991 by Eugene Beckham, John Sherrod and Craig Ronto. Reprinted with permission of Houghton Mifflin Harcourt Publishing Company. All rights reserved.

Illustrations from A FIELD GUIDE TO MUSHROOMS by Kent H. McKnight and Vera B. McKnight. Copyright © 1987 by Kent H. McKnight and Vera B. McKnight. Reprinted with permission of Houghton Mifflin Harcourt Publishing Company. All rights reserved.

Hassel, Karl.	Stream Before
Kasouth, George.	Mountains Before
KrzeSlak, Piotr ©123RF.com	Woods Before
Lee, Jason.	Ring neck snake
MacGregor, John.	Mountain chorus frog
Nardi, Jim.	Life in the Soil Graphic
Nedrelo, Dan.	Spotted salamander
Niemiller, Matthew L.	Green salamander
Noll, Paul.	Ruffed grouse
Peterman, Bill.	Five-lined skink; Slimy salamander
Petranka, Jim.	Marbled salamander
Pingleton, Mike.	Red-spotted newt
Sattler, Paul.	Jefferson salamander

Singer, Alan. The Estate of Arthur Singer. The following illustrations by Arthur Singer from A Guide to Field Identification, Birds of North America: Eastern screech owl, barred owl, whip-poor-will, pileated woodpecker, red-bellied woodpecker, ruby-crowned kinglet, cedar waxwing, blue-winged warbler, Northern parula, black-throated blue warbler, black-throated green warbler, cerulean warbler, yellow-throated warbler, blackburnian warbler, Kentucky warbler, hooded warbler, American redstart, Northern oriole, scarlet tanager, rose-breasted grosbeak, purple finch and broad-winged hawk.

Stockman, Vivian.	Mountains After, Woods After,
Speicher, Kim.	Corn snake
Thies, Ryan.	Rough green snake
Williams, Ken.	Stream After

www.ingramcontent.com/pod-product-compliance
Lightning Source LLC
Chambersburg PA
CBHW070615300426
44113CB00010B/1538